Posted Love | *new zealand love letters*

Posted Love | *new zealand love letters*

Sophie Jerram

PENGUIN BOOKS

To both Mary Jerram and Evžen Novak, whose love and letters have revived, sustained and inspired me at crucial moments.

PENGUIN BOOKS

Penguin Books (NZ) Ltd,
cnr Airborne and Rosedale Roads, Albany,
Auckland 1310, New Zealand
Penguin Books Ltd, 27 Wrights Lane,
London W8 5TZ, England
Penguin Putnam Inc, 375 Hudson Street,
New York, NY 10014, United States
Penguin Books Australia Ltd,
487 Maroondah Highway, Ringwood,
Australia 3134
Penguin Books Canada Ltd, 10 Alcorn
Avenue, Toronto, Ontario,
Canada M4V 3B2
Penguin Books (South Africa) Pty Ltd,
5 Watkins Street, Denver Ext 4, 2094,
South Africa
Penguin Books India (P) Ltd,
11, Community Centre, Panchsheel Park,
New Delhi 110 017, India

Penguin Books Ltd, Registered Offices:
Harmondsworth, Middlesex, England

First published by Penguin Books (NZ)
Ltd, 1999

1 3 5 7 9 10 8 6 4 2

Copyright © text, Sophie Jerram, 1999
Copyright © letters with individual collections

The right of Sophie Jerram to be identified
as the author of this work in terms of
section 96 of the Copyright Act 1994 is
hereby asserted.

Images on pages 23, 65, 109 and 139 from
New Zealand Post archives with thanks.
Copyright © New Zealand Post

Designed and typeset by Athena Sommerfeld

Printed in Australia by Australian Print
Group, Maryborough

All rights reserved. Without limiting the
rights under copyright reserved above,
no part of this publication may be
reproduced, stored in or introduced into
a retrieval system, or transmitted, in any
form or by any means (electronic,
mechanical, photocopying, recording or
otherwise), without the prior written
permission of both the copyright owner
and the above publisher of this book.

Every effort has been made to locate
all copyright holders. In the event that
notification has been inadvertently omitted,
the publisher would be grateful to hear
from the copyright holder, and will amend
following editions.

[contents]

acknowledgements | 8

foreword | 9

introduction | 10

beginnings | 23

    To the Queen of Loveliness | 24

    Soft-hearted girl | 25

    Dear Miss Waller | 26

    Toss to Edith | 28

    Cold as I look – Spencer Medley to Mary Taylor | 30

    Pokarekare Ana | 32

    Coded love | 34

    Hondo Hondo – Emily Deighton and Odo Strewe | 36

Harry Scott to Margaret Bennett | 46

A very serious question — James to Harriet | 48

Arthur Gibson to Annie Chew | 50

I want to bury myself like Alice | 52

Sophie Ode to Chris Brougham | 53

We should seemingly break off
 — John Prendeville to Amelia Monaghan | 54

Archie to Lois Little | 56

Bramwell Cook to Dorothy Money | 58

66 Courtney Place | 60

Ian to Fay, Johannesburg 1953 | 62

For the last time in our single lives
 — Ernest Hobbs to Lily Macdonald | 64

journeys | 65

Donald to Susan McLean | 66

Susan to Donald | 67

Annie Hill to Anna Richmond | 68

Just over 17 hours since we parted — Brian to Heather Barker | 70

Brent and Sally | 72

Ours is the God given pure love — Les Jerram to Vera | 74

You are my life — Len Douglas | 76

Hōri Hōrama to William Colenso | 78

If I were to cease to love you I would cease to be happy
 — Thomas King | 80

I want ... to get over the 'preliminaries' and live together a little
 — Katherine Mansfield to Leslie Beauchamp | 82

Joe to Zane | 84

Birthday scoldings — Mary Caroline Taylor to Mary | 86

'A' to 'P' — 20th-century email | 88

Chris Kraus — *I Love Dick* | 89

Mac to Nancy | 92

Dorothy to Douglas Gibbs | 93

Frilly feet | 94

On the tramp – James to Harriet Crooks | 96

Ern to Jenny Beaglehole | 98

Lumpy porridge | 100

God's will be done – Thomas to Grace Hirst | 102

Into the sea | 104

Lilian to Jack Elworthy | 107

endings | 109

Bob, Bil and Mery | 110

Charles Perrin, on death | 112

Scarlet fever delirium – Mary to James Richmond | 116

Anne to John Wilson, 1837 | 118

An Arctic glass bear | 120

Hamley diary | 121

Hongi to William Yate | 122

Shirley to Lester Lye | 124

Owen to Irene Jensen | 126

I was hardly a 'good catch' – Michael to Yvonne Edwards | 128

Go on in your ordinary life | 131

Peter Fraser to Harold Kemp | 136

Wild Flowers for Charles B | 138

epilogue | 139

On love letters – Mary Gallagher | 140

further reading | 142

endnotes | 143

[acknowledgements]

Posted Love is largely indebted to the staff of the Gallery of the National Library of New Zealand for their work in assembling the exhibition 'Posted Love', in particular Jill Trevelyan, without whom my task would have been many times larger. Thanks also to the Alexander Turnbull Library, in particular Margaret Calder, for permission to make much of this material available for publishing, also David Retter, Steven Chrisp and Margareta Gee.

Jo Benseman and Paul Ward as researchers were brilliant, and both unnerved at the enormity of our task. Thank you! Lucy Jerram provided much appreciated, gentle advice and assistance at tight moments. Thank you to Ingrid Horrocks for her skilled eye. My partner, the wonderful Evžen Novak, tolerated the late-night tensions and kept a quiet, interested eye on the whole project right through. The incorrigible, blessed Jo Randerson, who designed 'Posted Love' the exhibition, and who has been an inspiration and a believer in the entire project from the beginning, constantly rectified the spirit at crucial moments. I am also grateful for Charlotte Macdonald and Frances Porter's book *My Hand Will Write What My Heart Dictates,* which makes fascinating the stories of the intimate lives of 19th-century New Zealand women. This book could not have happened without the generosity and willingness of the letters' contributors to whom I am extremely grateful.

Finally, I am enormously appreciative of this wonderful opportunity provided to me by Penguin Books, with special thanks to Bernice Beachman, Philippa Gerrard and designer Athena Sommerfeld.

[foreword]

posted love

Posted Love was born from the exhibition 'Posted Love, Love Letters from the Turnbull Library and beyond', a project conceived and proposed to the National Library Gallery, Wellington, in late 1997. The exhibition ran between April and July 1999. In the research for the exhibition, we started with letters from the priceless collections of the Alexander Turnbull Library. I aimed to supplement these predominantly 19th-century letters with contemporary material by calling for contributions from the public through the news media from November 1998 to January 1999. It was an experiment that could have failed miserably; but it didn't and I am extremely grateful to those who, like me, wanted to share with others expressions of emotion that are sometimes overlooked in New Zealanders.

[introduction]

No other eyes than thine, my love, will see these lines, I have therefore no wish to disguise a single feeling ... Thomas King to Mary King, 10 June 1854

I discovered my first love letter when I was about 11, rummaging through an older sister's dressing-table drawer in search of chocolate. She was a well-known hoarder. The letter was from her recently departed boyfriend, a battered note on school refill pad in varying colours of ink saying what, I cannot remember. But I recall the sense of extreme intrigue and shock at having found such an intimate memento of their relationship, one which up to this point had only been nominal for me.

The realm of love letters is intensely private. And by the nature of their subject matter, many beautiful love letters will stay in the private realm, or become resigned to the fireplace. So those that have become available through the generosity of writers (or the coercion, enthusiasm or coercive enthusiasm of their families), or through donations made to the Turnbull Library are all the more extraordinary. To share one's personal writing requires a confidence, a security of faith, perhaps a foolhardiness. The act of revealing one's intimate thoughts within a country like New Zealand, all the more so, New Zealand's community being so small. Once the letters are 'outed', however, this small-worldness works to the collective advantage; our notion of being one big community makes reading other people's letters like reading your sister's diary, but with her permission. Despite emerging social differences, 1999 finds us still together, a messy, entangled family with all the sibling rivalry that comes with it.

Posted Love is no academic tome of history or literature, but neither is it written with a soft pink focus. What has led me to this book is my interest in the personal telling of stories about New Zealand. I am fascinated by the change in pace of love over time as reflected in these letters and the effects of technology on the communication of feelings. I also have an interest in what these letters might then say about New Zealand as a nation.

[between the lovers' covers]

It is being said that we are now entering the 'attention economy'.[1] An increased ability to communicate means that we are overwhelmed with information, consumed by choice, and have an increasing need to be able to tell the relevant from the peripheral. Those who can capture the most attention will be the most powerful. And in this context, it is possible to see that the love letter has always been a useful tool for capturing attention. Precisely targeted, candid where much communication is not, intimate and usually relevant only to the recipient, the love letter is an ideal device for gaining 'attention'. Increasingly, the news media are subscribing to and using the cult of personality: the intimate detailings of our political leaders, film stars and sports heroes sit alongside stories of war and peace. It is as if the human stories tell us more about our world than grand attempts at summing up the global political environment. The immediacy and captive power of the love letter coupled with this thirst for intimate knowledge of others makes the love letter an ideal viewing frame from which to understand our past and present worlds.

This being the case, *Posted Love* allows us a look at the intimate writings of some of those people who have contributed to New Zealand law and society. For example, we can see behind the scenes of three former New Zealand Members of Parliament. Thomas King (1821–1893) was known as a dry and reserved politician but the discovery of his vast collection of letters to his wife Mary points to his being one of the most eloquent and expressive writers of 19th-century New Zealand (see page 80). I am thankful to Margot Fry for introducing me to the writings of Thomas King. James Richmond (1820–1875) had just been made a cabinet minister in 1865 when he declared to his wife, Mary, that he would never again leave her for a long stretch of time (see page 116). She died before he could fulfil his commitment. Former Prime Minister Peter Fraser (1884–1950) wrote a letter to his stepson, Harold, revealing extraordinary sentiment on the death of Harold's mother, Janet, Fraser's adored wife (see page 136). Fraser was clearly aware of the potential of his letter to become public; there is a certain constructed style to his writing; he was writing on Prime Ministerial letterhead but he maintains a sincerity throughout.

Another figure of the nineteenth century was Captain William Lyon (1825–1887). While leading the Waikato Militia in the Land Wars of the 1860s, he cultivated a particularly close interest in his wife's clothing and appearance. When the discovery of his letters was made and then presented to the Turnbull Library, a number of military historians were alerted. When the letters were examined, however, they were found to show his command of the latest Auckland fashions rather than of his military battalion. How might this have affected Captain Lyon's military strategy (see page 94)?

The earliest letter in *Posted Love* was written in 1830; the latest in 1998. This span effectively covers New Zealand's recorded history. Unlike older nations, we are lucky still to have our time before us, to get things right, to learn from others' mistakes, to keep our best letters. Katherine Mansfield, usually claimed by the English, is probably the most famous New Zealand letter writer, and her fine writings have been recognised and saved, making her immortal.[2] May many more eloquent letter writers be treated likewise.

Formal New Zealand history tells us mostly of pioneering people and noble warriors. We have few tales of great love. Māori mythology contains stories of love but these are mostly presented as waiata (song) and oral history. Māori expressions of love in letter form are not commonly found. One of the few early examples of Māori letter writing is a letter written to the missionary William Colenso expressing the writer's dedication to God and to Colenso himself (see page 78). I am also privileged in being able to include one of the greatest song legends of New Zealand, 'Pokarekare Ana', which refers to itself metaphorically as a letter (see page 32).

[on new zealand love]

What distinguishes a New Zealand letter? Does anything mark out these letters as New Zealand in style? One new migrant, Flo Derry, pens her thoughts on how she wants to be thought of as a New Zealander:

Amuri, North Canterbury, New Zealand; 1855
You say you feel scared writing as you don't know whether you will please me, girls being such peculiar cattle. I think you said persons but nevermind one is objectionable as the other I take it. Well I'll tell you how to please me treat me exactly as if my name was John, Dick or Jack and I sported a decent little moustache. You can by doing so keep all your nice compliments honeyed speeches etc for the jolly nice English girls you know. By the way I may as well tell you I don't much admire English girls ... I much prefer a rowdy Colonial. Some colonials are every bit as stiff and starched as House girls, but the generality are pretty free and easy.
Flo Derry to Cousin Harry in Oxford, England[3]

If letters from prominent members of society say something about New Zealand then so do those from the less famous. In *Posted Love* you will find a remarkably diverse assortment of writers. Each letter, when I encountered it, felt like an individual gift. The letters possess a quality that neither speech nor gesture can relay. There is a mixture of letters: some philosophical, others with an appealing simplicity. In the selection of letters, I was looking for stories, for evidence of the deep waters underneath the still surface of the New Zealand psyche, and letters that are more of emotion rather than formal courtesy. Once writing a letter might have been purely a sign of etiquette. Yet I have selected those letter writers whose intention to communicate what they felt, whose inarticulation or effortless emotion is evident.

In other cases, the writer's oddity appealed, as in the case of young Charles Perrin who had an obsession with suicide. Archie Hull is another wonderful case. In the Turnbull Library, where we (the research team) first began our investigations and research, Hull's letters had been catalogued under 'love letters', yet after a good day's reading, we found his near-indecipherable prose dry, mundane and passionless. It was only after some persistence that we encountered the letter included here, one that reads so very touchingly, one of the most genuine letters of the entire collection. I like Archie Hull very much. I like his fallibility; his inconsistency. He is real.

One of the first letters we discovered that has not lost any of its poignancy is Spencer Medley's letter to his fiancée, Mary (see page 30). In 1861 he wrote:

Yes, you dear little Dove, cold as I look, quiet as I know I seem, I have a very soft heart, you soon took it away, you can depend on keeping it, if it's worth your while.

Yet the restraint and notions of propriety that middle-class colonials had supposedly left behind still confused them in their new country. Mary, forever being castigated by her mother for her naughty behaviour (see page 86), was still grappling with what was right and proper, while Spencer urged her to be upfront with her communications with him:

Take courage darling, don't think too much of what the world thinks of you. Depend upon it, we are not talked about so much as our consciousness would lead us to imagine ...

Mary's apparent self-consciousness may be a clue to the essence of New Zealand for you will find ample evidence that some people find it easier to write words of love than to say them. The most undemonstrative of New Zealand men and women are shown in *Posted Love* writing the most profound and emotional words. Many contributors of letters were amazed that their friends, fathers, mothers and lovers had it in them to write so candidly. Some contributors commented that their relatives never opened their hearts except on paper.

To my surprise, the research for *Posted Love* revealed more letters written by men than by women. The high proportion of men's letters to women's may be evidence that men feel more comfortable documenting, as opposed to speaking, their passions than women. Or it may simply be that women are better archivists of these emotional gems from their lovers, husbands, sons or fathers.

As an exception to this, the missionary William Yate was one of the better-known collectors of his received letters, publishing a book in 1835, *An Account of New Zealand; and of the formation and progress of the Church Missionary Society's Mission in the Northern Island*.[4] It includes a number of letters from Māori, including one from Yate's former lover, Hongi. Yate was later dismissed from the Church Missionary Society because of his sexual relationships with several young Māori men. Hongi writes to Yate on Yate's return to England in 1830:

You say you shall return; but I am thinking, no: you will not leave again your good country, for this bad country, and this very bad and unbelieving people. You will love your own friends more than the New Zealanders, and will not again leave them for this ... Go in peace, Mr Yate, and see your friends in Europe; and say How-do-you-do to the whole of them, not passing over one ... (see page 122)

[time, technology]

June 3 1823

We have been sent your dispatches from England dated Sept and though our hearts were gladdened, our appetites have ever since craved for more — your letters were most exhilarating and came at a time when we wanted a little cordial. Marianne Williams, missionary, to family [5]

Travelling between New Zealand and Britain in the 1820s would take approximately three to four months. A letter could take much longer. The length of time between writing and receiving a letter could be nine months. In 1999, an email can take seconds. The email arrives from a loved one and a reply is expected within minutes. Are we able to mine our hearts for profound declarations of love before our 'email etiquette' credits are exhausted?

One email romance started in May 1998 between Wellington and Auckland lovers was consummated and finished by November 1998. Relationships conducted in such a virtual way have run their course in the time that an initial letter of friendship might have taken to arrive in the 19th century. Our ability to scan, search and test-drive the ideal partner is increased thanks in part to the telecommunications industry.

Imagined pleasure and the suspense of embrace seem to me to make the best love letters. There is something about the distance and patience of our amorous forebears that made the anticipation of their eventual union somewhat heightened as they savoured early connections or lingered over touches.

Archie Hull enjoyed his courtship with Lois Little (see page 56) in 1940:

I have just fished out of a pocket a handkerchief with a trace of lipstick on it and a faint smell of your perfume. How extraordinarily potent such little things like that are in establishing a contact between us, not that there isn't one all the time now… There have been times quite often when we cannot look at each other without feeling our hearts will burst but never so much as on Saturday & Sunday … To be so close to beauty was of itself the most perfect thing that I have ever known, you are so very lovely Lois and yet all your beauty of body and beauty of soul is only part, though the greatest part of the bigger thing we call our love.[6]

And Ernest Hobbs' writing encapsulated the patience of the fiancé, when he wrote to Lily (see page 64) two days before their marriage in 1913:

Of course I know you have always loved me sweetheart but only as a lover, but the time is almost at hand when you can love me with a love that only a wife can know ... I remain your loving sweetheart until Wednesday ...[7]

Even well into marriage, the well-crafted letter can persuade, allude and excite. As a tangible memento, it can exist as an erotic substitute for the writer. The physicality of the letter attempts to replace the connection between lovers. Thomas King injects the viscerality of his desire into his letters to his wife throughout their marriage. King's letters constantly refer to his physical reaction to her presence or absence.

How in the lone nights I feel the blood coursing through my veins when your image rises before me ...

When I am with you I can tell you much that I dare not pen, much that the tongue dares not utter, that the eye and lip of love can alone reveal ...

When I close my eyes I conjure up your dear form. I see my Polly's rosy cheeks, her ruddy lips, her gentle grey eyes. I cannot feel the rapture which her sweet lips and fond embraces can impart, but I can love her and paint her as I will.[8]

The letter has changed from being a compulsory observance of good society, to an optional method of expression. That we now rely upon the ubiquitous typeface and immediacy of telecommunications for expressing our thoughts and feelings to the detriment of the art of letter writing is an easy conclusion. In transcription, language that once would have been encoded in spidery writing is suddenly released from its shackles by the access to type. The words are now available to many and, in being so, they gain a democratic authority. But a degree of beauty is lost in this democratic conversion. Reduced to bare words, text loses the personal power imbued by handwriting.

'Is letter writing dying?' is the most frequently asked question I have been posed on the subject of the love letter. Attempting to deal with the same issue in 1976, Antonia Fraser writes '... letters can be carried around as talismans to refresh the memory where love (telephone) calls can merely be recollected in tranquillity, and the memory may not refresh them'.[9]

But it is now 1999; fax and email have arrived and life is faster. It is my view that it is not letter writing that is dying, but patience, persistence and the pleasure of anticipation. We are perhaps more hungry to taste the flesh than to linger over a gradually blossoming relationship. We have trouble waiting for the postman.

There are those who will always savour the letter, and those who will succumb to the buzz of technology. I see little point in mourning change. In a 1998 postcard to 'Meg', 'Adrienne' puts it well:

How can we triumph over the telephone tyrant? How can thousands of miles of optic fibre replace the hand, the eye, the breath and the magic of presence? Your writing bridges the gap to some extent. It does emanate a deeper you.[10]

[posted love]

Posted Love began as a question: Are New Zealanders as capable of heartfelt passion as those romantic cultures who are famous for their display of love? And if so, is it a passion worthy of public admission? I was living in Italy in 1996 when this proposition struck me. I was surrounded by strangers willing to share their anger and tears with me; by an atmosphere of drama that made going to the supermarket or the letterbox an event worthy of dressing up and putting on lipstick. I had never felt this degree of exposed emotion before. Do all cultures feel this degree of desire, of outrage, of melancholy? I wondered if it were just the mode of expression, rather than our feelings that are different? This book is an attempt at an answer, though these are not questions that will be resolved easily.

Posted Love has been structured as a story might be. The first section, Beginnings, contains stories of early love, of courtship, of the art of escaping the disapproving parent. Watch for the first-time elocutor, the stumbling, swooning youth. See how the letters of less mature writers sometimes say more about the writer than they do about the lover. Notice how proposals of marriage are distinct from or blurred with early declarations of new-found heartache.

The second section, Journeys, comprises letters of love more fully shaped; love that lasts, or splutters on rough roads. Here are the difficult 'tough love' letters of parents to children, and those of reflection and gratitude for love that has continued. I am sorry not to be able to include, for want of space, the reflections and pledges of renewed commitment shown in numerous collections of annual wedding-anniversary letters.

The last section, Endings, is about the contemplation of death, finality and completion – final moments and goodbyes. The letters are mixed chronologically – I believe that love has no sense of time, but only of pace. May you feel the reassurance that things change; and that there will always be new love. As someone dies, another person is falling in love. So if at the end you find sadness creeping over you, remember that *Posted Love* was not intended for maudlin thoughts and funereal faces. Do read *Posted Love* backwards as well as forwards.

Someone came up to me in the street the other day and said: 'I wrote a letter in your exhibition. Thank you – it worked!' My private hope is that *Posted Love* will inspire more exquisite letter writing. The letter can survive where life does not. The letter may be able to say what we could not during our lifetime or reinforce that which could be forgotten at the time of conflict or death. And tomorrow's memory will only be sustained by writing today.

Sophie Jerram
August 1999

a wide-awake numbed paralysed and unrelievable joy | beginnings

> To the Queen of Loveliness
>
> This letter was written to Maida Julian by her cousin Ronald prior to one of their many jaunts in the country around Stratford and Mount Egmont (Taranaki). Their relationship was not known to be romantic. Maida married a Mr Govenlock a few years later. Ronald, unfortunately, perished in a mining accident in Taranaki in the 1930s.
>
> COLLECTION OF GOVENLOCK FAMILY

Portia St
Stratford
30/7/29

To Her Most Gracious Majesty
The Queen of Lovliness

Your most humble and devoted subject begs to offer your Majesty the use of his limousine and the attendance of his all too unworthy person on the occasion of your projected visit next Saturday evening to the 'Countess of Downs.' Her ladyship has expressed herself as delighted at the prospective visit, so I will do myself the honour of attending your Majesty as soon as the preoccupations of the day are dispensed with, say about the hour of 6.30 p.m. If fortune smiles on me I have presumed to think it not improbable that your Serene Highness may condescend to ask me to take a little light refreshment with the Queen Dowager and your most Illustrious Self before we face the perils of the road, so I will not wait for anything so mundane as food, but will use all dispatch to reach your August Presence. Gladly offering you my humble duty and fully acknowledging your most Glorious Sovereignty in the Realm of Lovliness.

I am, Most Gracious Lady
Yours to Command
Ronald, Baron Salisbury Earl of Tuna

Soft-hearted girl

This letter was written in 1998 by a 10-year-old Auckland boy to his first girlfriend. His feelings proved rather overwhelming for her and she was not responsive to his articulate verse. He now has another girlfriend who is 'more suitable' according to his mother.

COLLECTION OF COOPER FAMILY

Dear the most soft hearted, beautiful girl in the world,

Have you noticed that we have been together for almost one year now? I'm so so sorry that I haven't written in a very long time I feel so mean and bad. when we were playing Chinese whispers I noticed how pretty you were and how soft your hear is and how nice your happy laugh and smile were and releiased how lucky I was to be with you for ...

Dear Miss Waller

Thomas Jensen sent this proposal to Gwen Waller in 1930. Nothing is known as to how Gwen responded, but her suitor was evidently unsuccessful — Gwen married Bill Neas five years later.

COLLECTION OF JOHN NEAS

Omata Road, Westown
New Plymouth
January 31st. 1930

Dear Miss Waller

I am now in a position to let you know what I have long wished to tell you, of my feelings towards you — perhaps I should call it love. You may be pleased or upset or even unmoved but I don't think you'll be just that, but at anyrate I shall have lifted a weight off my chest and probably done the right thing. I cannot view the matter in any other light. It is my duty to myself to tell you. Ever since first I knew you I have loved you immensely but I felt that I could not tell you then, not through shyness so much, but on account of my connections with another girl. At present I don't think that I should be more explicit. I don't know what sort of an answer you'll give me but I'm prepared for the worst. I shall try to be almost equally happy with reverse as with success. Of course it will be hard but if you have no liking for me whatsoever it's no use. To my mind it would be a decided pity because I have nearly convinced myself already that we possess qualities agreeable to each other and that is the vital necessity isn't it. Of course that would require to be proved and for that very reason I would very much like to become much more intimately acquainted with you. I quite realise the real difficulties in the way but I think that correspondence and social contacts at opportune occasions would provide sufficient opportunity to discover the essential characteristics of each other. Be that as it may, I am pleading for something of that sort. Truly girls of your class are not so very common after all. I meet a fair number nowadays but they mostly seem so simple so uncultivated somehow — so lacking in those qualities so essentially girlish. I don't know whether you'll quite understand me — my composition is nothing marvellous. You must however appreciate the deep sincerity of this letter. I have plenty of that which is most essential and must have thousands in addition soon and if you would ever care to revisit New Plymouth and stay with us you should have a very happy time. In our way of living we are just ordinary people, perhaps a little proud but then we really have some occasion to be so. We have a new bungalow in Upper Westown. I really am saying altogether too much for a first letter especially as I only know you and nothing more but I'm willing to lay all my cards on the table, be frank, and try to appear before you at my true worth. I don't want to appear as a goody-good now, which I am not, and then let you discover something quite different later. I expect that you will answer with equal sincerity and openness if I know you aright and I shall be glad. If you feel that you cannot meet me say so, without entertaining sympathetic notions. I should have liked very much to have had a heart to heart talk with you during the Summer School but no really suitable occasion seemed to present itself. Probably my initiative is not what it should be. Be quite friendly and confident in your reply, address me just as you please. You may be very sure that your confidence will be respected whatever be the nature of that reply.

Believe me to be
Very sincerely yours
Thomas A Jensen

Toss to Edith

When Toss Woollaston married Edith Alexander in 1936 he was just beginning his career as a painter and had little hope of earning a living from his art. He died in 1998, a well-respected and eminent painter. It was said: 'Toss's death can be described as the end of a grand era for the visual arts in this country.'[11]

Toss wrote of his relationship with Edith:[12] 'One of Rodney Kennedy's aunts said she was a fool to marry me, I had no money. Nobody said I was a fool to marry her, though she had none either. Her father, the City Engineer of Dunedin, gave her neither an allowance nor a dowry ...

'The way she supported me in my painting, then, was by her faith in it. Not till after we had been married thirty years did it bring in a living. During that time we raised a family on my earnings as, successively, an orchard worker, a factory hand, and a Rawleigh's salesman. She was undemanding in the womanly matter of new clothes. Her social life, with few exceptions, was confined to the family. She shared the hardships of our life without complaint.'

The following letter was written by Toss to Edith during their courtship.

COLLECTION OF THE MUSEUM OF NEW ZEALAND, TE PAPA TONGAREWA. WITH KIND PERMISSION OF THE TRUSTEES OF THE TOSS WOOLLASTON ESTATE

Dunedin 1936
C/- Mrs A. Kennedy
73 Somerville St
Andersons Bay

Edith,

Realisation that I am in love with you has struck me with a wide-awake numbed paralysed and unrelievable joy — so that I feel as if it were pain really.

Last night when you ran back I wanted to embrace you and kiss you for relief of it — and went home remorseful for my bungling.

I am like a great sail suddenly taut with a strong gust — but below me is a leaden ship resisting.

I hope we are not both going to be imprisoned in your indefiniteness!

You were beautiful last night — at moments I longed intensely to be painting you.

I will try and get this to you this morning — Saturday.

Toss.

Cold as I look — Spencer Medley to Mary Taylor

This letter was written to Mary Taylor by her fiancé, Lieutenant Spencer Medley, aide-de-camp to Governor Grey. The two were married in 1863. Spencer Medley died in 1893 and Mary in 1922, aged 87.

Mary Taylor was the daughter of the Rev. Richard Taylor and his wife, Mary Caroline. See also the letter Mary Caroline wrote to Mary on her 11th birthday in 1846 (page 86).

MANUSCRIPTS AND ARCHIVES COLLECTION, ALEXANDER TURNBULL LIBRARY MS-PAPERS-3762-2/1

27 April 1861

My own darling Meri

It is only two hours since I bundled off two letters, one for you and one for your father — I was very much hurried at the end of it, and as I shall never tire of chattering, teasing, lecturing and otherwise boring you by letter, so I ask you to put up with it all, and to forgive all my little misdemeanours, and my very evident blunders ...

I want you darling to give up (don't let it be a pang) the idea of writing through Lady Martin — what does it matter dear. Everyone knows of our engagement. Then what harm in directing to Spencer Medley. Surely there is nothing unmaidenly in that and you cannot be ashamed of the name of Medley, for it will belong to you some day. Take courage darling, don't think too much of what the world thinks of you. Depend upon it, we are not talked about so much as our consciousness would lead us to imagine ...

I went to Government House in the evening — I enjoyed myself very much — just a quiet family evening ... Miss Cherry very kindly sung the whole evening, and with so much good nature & good grace and also with great expression and taste. She sung that curious wild song 'The three fishers' and many others ... in many of which my thoughts fled back in repose into that dear little nest of love which you have made in the innermost recep of my heart — Yes, you dear little Dove, cold as I look, quiet as I know I seem, I am afraid I have a very soft heart, you soon took it away, you may depend on keeping it, if it's worth your while ...

God bless you darling
Ever your very loving
Spencer

Pokarekare Ana

Paraire Henare Tomoana wrote this song for his wife to be, Kuini Ripeka Ryland, in April 1912. Written as a love letter put to music, 'Pokarekare Ana' has become one of the most well-known and popular songs of Aotearoa/ New Zealand.

Paraire Henare Tomoana was a prolific writer and composer, and most of his songs covered a range of love themes. Other songs he wrote were 'E Pari Ra', and 'Tahi nei taru kino'. He died in 1946.

WITH KIND PERMISSION OF NGATAI HUATA (GRANDDAUGHTER OF THE LATE PARAIRE HENARE TOMOANA). TEXT AND TRANSLATION PROVIDED BY THE CHILDREN OF PARAIRE & KUINI

Pokarekare ana	As the rippling waters of Waiapu
nga wai o Waiapu	Break against its banks
Whiti atu koe, e hine	But subside into calmness
Marino ana e	When you pass over My Love
E Hine e	Oh my Beloved
Hoki mai ra	Please come back to me
Ka mate ahau	For I will surely die
I te aroha e	Of my love for you
Tuhituhi taki reta	I have written this letter
Tuku atu taku ringi	I have sent my ring
Kia kite to Iwi	Should your people see them
E raruraru ana e	There may be trouble
E Hine e	My Beloved

Hoki mai ra	Come back to me
Ka mate ahau	My heart is breaking
I te aroha e	For you My Love
Kua whati taku pene	My pen is broken
Kua pau aku pepa	My paper is gone
Ko taku aroha	However my beloved
E manu tonu ana e	My love is eternal
E Hine e	Oh Maiden
Hoki mai ra	Return to me
Ka mate ahau	For I am dying
I te aroha e	Of my love for you
E kore te aroha	The sun's hot rays
E maroke i te ra	Will not sear my love for you
Makuku tonu	But instead will be kept evergreen
Aku roimata e	By my falling tears
E Hine e	Oh my dear Beloved
Hoki mai ra	Come back to me
Ka mate ahau	For my heart is breaking
I te aroha e	For love of you
E Hine e	Dear heart of mine
Hoki mai ra	I will wait for thee
Ka mate ahau	My love is thine alone
I te aroha e	For eternity

33
beginnings

Coded love

Amelia Webb's parents ordered her to write to Nicholas Loye and tell him 'never to darken their doorstep again'. She wrote the letter, gained the approval of her parents, and hastily added the postscript before sealing the envelope. Amelia and Nicholas were married three months later in 1860 in Whitehills, Bendigo, Australia, and emigrated to New Zealand in 1862.

COLLECTION OF ALAN LOYE

Dear Nicholas

The great love I have hitherto expressed to you
Is false, and I find my indifference towards you
Increases daily. The more I see of you the more
You appear in my eyes an object of contempt.
I feel myself in every way disposed and determined
To hate you. Believe, I never had any intention
To offer you my hand. Our last conversation has
Left a tedious reality which has by no means
given me the most exalted idea of your character.
Your temper would make me extremely unhappy
And if we are united I shall experience nothing but
the hatred of my parents added to the everlasting dis-
pleasure in living with you. I have indeed a heart
to bestow, but do not desire you to imagine it
at your wish, I could not give it to any one more
inconsistant and capacious than you are and less
capable to do honour to my choice and family.
Yes, I hope you will be persuaded that
I speak sincerely and you will do me a favour
to avoid me. I shall excuse you taking the trouble
to answer this, your letters are always full of
impertinence and you have not the shadow of
wit and good sense. Adieu, adieu believe me I am
so adverse to you that it is impossible for me ever
to be your affectionate friend and humble servant,
Yours A

P.S. After reading this please read it again, missing every second line.

Hondo Hondo — Emily Deighton and Odo Strewe

Odo Strewe was born in Germany in 1910 and left late in 1937 to escape the Nazi regime. After travelling through Canada, Hawaii and Fiji, where he met Emily Deighton (Amy), Odo settled in New Zealand. The following two letters are part of a close correspondence maintained over five years. In 1944 Amy's brother wrote to Odo to ask him to terminate his correspondence with Amy who was due to be married. Nothing further is known about Amy. During World War II, Odo was interned at Somes Island with other 'aliens', and after his release in 1946, he worked as a journalist. He later married and had four children. Throughout an extraordinary life Odo inspired the passionate writing and attentions of many women.

STREWE COLLECTION, MANUSCRIPTS AND ARCHIVES COLLECTION, ALEXANDER TURNBULL LIBRARY
MS-GROUP-0563, WITH KIND PERMISSION OF OLIVER STREWE

Odo Strewe C.C. P.O. Titirangi. Auckland. N.Z.

AMY

Februar, 4.th. 1939

Odo Strewe C.C. P.O. Titirangi. Auckland. N.Z.

Februar, 4.th. 1939

37 beginnings

Thanks for your interesting letter from the 18th. Deec. A rearly very good letter or piece of thought. I never could imagine that my little girlfriend (sweet little girlfriend) had such possibilities to express herself. Bravo to you. But dont worry about me. I am such a funny person so of orginality that I am moving on tracks whom to other people seem absurd. But caused through my Weltschmerz, unbalanced responsibility, phantsatic principles on one occasion or none on another, phantastic longings and to much logig to see throug – through myself. But so mixed with some more strongly developed passions I may bee develope to a 'not bade' writer.

Jes the islands. There is nothing in the world that has ever so entangled, so embraced, so disturbed me, rocked in sadness and happiness as this dream I had somewhere in the continent and realising its existence : islands.

To right you are, Nature is grand (just grand). But why do you speak of the simplicity of Nature? Nothing is a greater riddle to us than Nature. And what is not Nature???

Even Decadense is Nature. Cause and effect are natural principles. But dont ask me of the sense of live? Yes the relative truth is selfpreservation. From this angle may be truth dont is much more so relative. But the "right" way in keeping self preservation going "Ah" there again starts the game "who is who" I mean who is right.

Certainley I will return to the islands and if this blessed war didn' started I would be allready "somewhere" on the islands. But to much knowledge my dear is never a hindernis (is that english?) I mean a barricade to apprecciate the life on the islands. Opposite philosophical world conception makes longing to live and to die on the islands. I understand your writings very clearly my dear Amy. And I would not wonder if you one day became a very good writer. That a compliment but I mean it. This lousy capitalistic system, Production for profit instead for consumption the root of all evil. Please would you give me a defination of the word "soul" I can't. To bade that I cannot talk to you this damned writing makes me all silly. Speaking — a million words I could throuw over you. So its just a stammering with a typewriter. Now then — the main aim of love is — again — selfpreservation. The preservation of the species. Je! You got quite exited above the former sweetheard of mine and her opinion of love. So she wasn't so wrong. Take an animal. The time comes for copulation. The exciting is growing until the moment cuts it off through an orgasm. That's pure biological. The same with mankind. The second strongest instinct or motion is after the hunger, the sex. Now man behave like animal too right — my symphies for women are greater as for man. — Monagamie — that mean running with a female for all the time is quite unnatural on our hole globe. When men became higher developed (formertimes men were also pollygame) and the state became higher developed they invented the marriage certificate and the word ethik. My cat sends her regards.

You speak of simplicity of Nature. What I have defined is simplicity, what you are speaking of is allready high developed mindelove Love not only out of sexual instinkt. Love mental comeradshipe, harmonie in thought and other stuff. You write "And Sex

is also beautiful as in it's true sense it is the expression of the feelings of the heart."
Sex is beautiful, jes if it would not be human — animal and plant live that mean all
zoological and botanic live would die out. That's one of the tricks of nature!!!
"Feelings of the heart" No — sex is the expression of the production of the hormone
glance. A castrated man never loves. Not even with "the heart". What about reading
Darwin, Mendel, Molleschott, Büchner, Häckel, and H.G. Wells "The sience of live"
is also not bade. My "beloved" Amy you are kicking to many high browed words
around. I never said Love is the combination of soul and sex. I neveruse the word
soul. But so my outlook on love might hurt the most peoples impressions it is much
more truthfull as all that romantik blubber. And what is more truthful is mor
beautiful...

What about the pleasant surprise? I am rearly tortured — I am so inquisitive — what
can it be??? I dont now. But you must send anything important REGISTERED.

In the last letter I got the 5 bob for the voice but rearly you should send it registered.

If you like I grow on the "desert island" a beard.

You are not interested in the squabbles of the various nations. But Amy — W A R is
not just a squabbles its a cruel dirty filthy horror. Where are your humane feelings.
Brotherhood and the other high spoken words? Tomorrow the war is may be near
your place. To long, were the people not interested and they wonder when they get
butshered.

Now my island girl, so I have not agreed with your writing in all points so it shows
a scale of wonderful thinking. Just go on and study, study, study.

Ca moce Daulomani xxx Your Odo

Please write soon Odo.

Your letter Hond[o]

happy, a sensation of tremblin[g]

feeling of such happiness surg[ed]

should write me such a lovely

proud. Hondo, my Darling, wer[e]

in extacy at your feet.

Government Stores,
Suva.
27th Feb. 1940

Your letter Hondo Hondo, it caused me to be happy, a sensation of trembling, of a desire to weep — a feeling of such happiness surged through my being. That you should write me such a lovely letter I am very glad and proud. Hondo, my Darling, were you here I would just weep in extacy at your feet.

The NIAGARA arrived on Friday and I was longing intensely for a letter, but no' — Saturday passed, no letter. My disappointment was great. But when on Monday your letter came, my whole being just overflowed in the love I have for you.

I am pleased you liked my letter and think that 'someday' I may be a writer. I have commenced an article on Native Life. Of course, my style of writing at present is vague. So far I have written only four pages. Perhaps I have before mentioned that I wrote to the Regal Institute in London last year asking for information and they state that a Course in Short Story Writing costs £6/6/o. I think you should be proud of yourself having your article published. If ever I wrote any stuff that would be accepted I guess I'd go crazy with joy. It would be just grand if we were together and you could help me. I have been thinking very seriously of the advantages of living in N.Z. Firstly, I would be near you, then there are the libraries where one may gather information and ideas of good writers, also one could attend Night School for further education. Even if I came up for awhile, I am just dying to see you. I know you will not encourage this idea, I cannot understand why?. To my way of thinking this WAR will possibly last years and if we are going to be seperated all that time I think it will be <u>terrible.</u> Surely I could get work in Auckland in some office, or anyplace where they pay decently. What wages do they pay girls?. Or perhaps I could get into the Auckland hospital as a nurse?. Hondo Hondo, please agree to my coming to N.Z. We could both work together towards attaining our dream of returning to the islands to plant 'Dalo'. Of course, I have not lived in Auckland since I have grown up and therefore, do not know much about, the 'advantages or disadvantages' of living in a city. But, whatever you advise Hondo I know will be from a experienced point of view. Should you think it better for me to live in Suva. You MUST WRITE IN DETAIL OF THIS MATTER. But, I would so much love to come to you.

Your sentence "rocked in sadness and happiness" reads beautifully.

Well, Hondo, when I wrote 'Simplicity of Nature' I meant that in it's greatness lie simplicity. I cannot explain exactly the meaning of Simplicity but for example, a intelligent man will always welcome the company of small children — why? — because in the simple state of a child's mind, the intelligent mature brain .... No, Hondo I can find no words to express my meaning.

You have taught me "in that too much knowledge is not a hinderance. I understand your explanation. I will learn very much of life from you. But what exactly I meant is probably — insufficient knowledge. I mean, that there are so many people — the Mass, whom will jeer when one comments on the deep beauty of Nature, until you enlightened me, I thought that people whom do not appreciate Nature have become so clever, they find no longer any interest in Trees, sunsets etc. Perhaps, I confuse you with the wrong use of words. I thought the VOICE preached Anti-war. What exactly is Russia doing to Finland.?

Hondo Hondo, your memory failed you when you said you did not tell me that love is a combination of Soul and Sex. I am almost sure, you told me this. Recollect, when I said "Oh, you only want my body" This took place one night when we were coming back from Francis's place. You replied that Love is understanding of the mind and sex, works in, so that one is not without the other. Well, if you did not actually say "Combination of Soul and Sex it was Mind and Sex. My definition or the nearest explanation of Soul is, the Being, the fact of Life in us. Oh, hell, it is confusing but try and understand that a corpse has no soul. I suppose it is just another word for life. But then, what about the people in Tibet WHO STUDY SOUL-LIFE.?

I will try to get the books written by the various authors you have mentioned Hondo Hondo, but as you know, outstanding books are difficult to procure in Suva and the library is not well stocked.

You say I use high-brow words, but my Dear I do NOT think so. Sometimes, one is better able to express one's thoughts with (as You call high-brow words) to my mind they merely serve the purpose of expression better.

I will dream of our little grass shack and you singing. Of course, remember when you sang to me down at the wharf? I hope you like the job of planting Dalo, it is not very easy work. Yes, the desert island will be so cut-off from Suva, there will not be any barbers and long hair and a beard will look fine. Long hair, a

beard, a sulu and I will have my perfect Hondo Hondo. I will
wear a sulu and we will lie on mats, it will be just wonderful.

I am sending you a mat and a piece of 'tapa' this mail. Be sure
to ask at the post office for a large long white box. Try sleeping
on the mat instead of a sheet. I do sleep on a mat and it feels
lovely against one's body. By the way, did you receive the small
piece of tapa I sent last mail Hondo?

The surprise is the mat. Also I am enclosing £2 in case you may
be in desperate need of something. I am registering the letter.

I agree with you concerning "what is more truthful is more
beautiful".

I left the Agricultural Dept. sometime ago. I was transferred to
the Government Stores — most uninteresting. I have written to
the Director of Agriculture asking for information about the
Plantago Seed. As yet there has been no reply. Govt. Depts take
so long to do anything. I might have time to go and see them
before the mail closes. There are many native medicines here
which are excellent for constipation. The Fijians have some
really startling herbs for cures. My Mother is quite an expert
on Fijian medicines. The Plantago Seed sounds interesting.

Where are my human feelings? Well, perhaps if the Leaders
of the various countries possessed human feelings there would
be no War. War, to my mind, is rotten and everything you say
it is. The majority of the people choose their leaders and in

Yours,

choosing their leaders I expect they wish if necessary to fight for them. Of course, as we both agree, capitalism is at the root of it all. I am deeply sorry and troubled concerning War but what do you think I can do? Besides, judging from talks heard, there are heaps of men just dying to go to the war — they certainly do not want my sympathy ...

Do you still think the N.Z. people are sheep?

When we settle on our dalo patch you may write to your mother and ask her to come and eat with us. That would be swell.

Please write soon and tell me if it is wise to come to Auckland — I do so much want to come.

Sa Moce Daulomani,
Yours,
Amy

Be sure to write and tell me if you have received the Mat & 'Tapa'.
x x x
My weight is about 9 stones — you do not like fat girls do you? Why do you not send me a photo of yourself? I post this mail a book called "Story of My Heart" explaining 'Soul'.

Harry Scott to Margaret Bennett

Harry Scott wrote this letter to Margaret Bennett prior to their marriage. They had met in Christchurch in 1947, became engaged in 1949, and married the following year. They had three children. Harry died in a climbing accident on Mount Cook in 1953."

MANUSCRIPTS AND ARCHIVES COLLECTION, ALEXANDER TURNBULL LIBRARY MS-PAPERS-6309-01. WITH KIND PERMISSION OF MARGARET SCOTT.

11 pm
Darling —

I did not come in tonight to see you — not because it was too late, but because I love you too much. When I am with you it makes everything else so unreal, so real is our relationship. It makes going off to do anything — and especially coming home here by myself so bleak — I look forward to such partings with apprehension. So having got into a mood of serenity during the course of the evening — warmed by love, rather than immediately excited by it, I decided to let it go at that for the night. Forgive me this time — no doubt it cannot happen again.

Margaret, the reality and joy of your love, your eagerness and sweetness, your serenity, somehow invades me and makes me overwhelmed with happiness & thus the more impatient for next year. I wonder at it all — that you exist, that you should have been turned in my direction, that early on you could see more clearly and certainly than I fills me with gratitude.

The rain falls in the dark outside; somehow it is more still, and silence is deeper when I can hear the rain. Perhaps that is a parallel with the fact that I love all people more because so much is concentrated on you, dear child.

I love you my dear
H.

A very serious question — James to Harriet

James Crooks writes here to his fiancée, Harriet. Little is known about their courtship, but they emigrated to New Zealand from Scotland sometime prior to 1885 and settled in Petone. See page 96 for a letter from him during their life in New Zealand.

MANUSCRIPTS AND ARCHIVES COLLECTION, ALEXANDER TURNBULL LIBRARY
MS-PAPERS 2413

Doncaster
7th February 1875

My dear Harriet

I landed safe here last night about 1/2 past 12 o'clock it was rather a cold ride but as I took some Whiskey with me and the cold did me no harm.

I hope you were not any the worse of being out in the rain last night — the wetting I got did me no harm, unless it is the cause of the headache I have had most of the day — it might be but I don't think it is, as I have been very subject to them of late, hardly ever being without one — I hope you have thought over what I asked you last night as it is a very serious question as far as I am concerned if not for you also consider it carefully over before you make your mind up, as it is for eternity not only for this life but for the life to come also — as true love can never die — but the more it is tried the purer it becomes. If you make your mind up in my favour as I pray God you may, I hope you will forgive my selfish request in asking you to be <u>my wife</u> when there is George before me, but after thinking it over I could not see what I should or rather could not ask you for the greatest wish of my life. Oh that I had always thought so, it would have saved me a world of pain and suffering and you also it would have saved but I believe God had meant it to be as it is on purpose to show me what love is. Not only our love in this world, but what our love for him should be. And also that as I love you so, who is mortal how much more should I love christ who is immortal and who died for us. You may be astonished to see me write like this but the truth is that when I thought about you who are good and pure and wishing you for my stay in this life I was naturally led me to think of the life to come — I have no more time on hand just now so with love to all.

I am dear Harriet
Yours Ever

James K. Crooks

P.S. Remember its to be <u>Yes</u>. Excuse this scribble please

Arthur Gibson to Annie Chew

Arthur Henry Gibson was born in 1861 in Manchester, England. He emigrated to New Zealand in 1878 and until 1919 was involved mainly with farming ventures around the country. Annie Chew, the daughter of John Chew, and her family resided in a house called Millwood Crofton, in Ngaio, Wellington.

Arthur wrote this letter to his fiancée, Annie, when she was holidaying in Sydney before their marriage. Arthur had planned their wedding and his letters are filled with his longing for Annie's return. Arthur died in 1935, however no further information is known about his life with Annie.

MANUSCRIPTS AND ARCHIVES COLLECTION, ALEXANDER TURNBULL LIBRARY
MS-PAPERS-0401-20

Crofton N Zealand
4 April 1891 (9pm)
(raining heavily)

Darling Annie,

... <u>Tremendous</u> alterations have been made, my darling lady, since your departure, in the arrangements of this house. You will find you are no longer in 1 bed. <u>That</u> has been altered. I have also <u>got</u> a sponge bath for her dainty ladyship, into which every morning she <u>shall</u> go. I am also going to <u>try</u>, when you come back to get up fairly early and light the fire, so as to let you have a little warm water in the morning to wash with. I know Madam you are laughing at the very idea of my getting up early at any time. But give me a trial at all events, and then see if I can't wait upon you, and spare you a little drudgery.

You may laugh, but I should like you to <u>teach</u> me to wait upon you always. I love to hear you order me to do something for <u>you</u>. I am not joking when I say I have staked all upon your love for me, and upon our future happiness, and if I can succeed in making you really happy, and in leading you on to better things, I shall be more than content, for I shall not have lived in vain. I am going to give up friends and everything, and devote myself entirely to your service. So now, madam, can you love me just a <u>little</u> in return?

... And now darling goodbye and as many kisses as ever could be given in 30 minutes. And believe me your own true love
Arthur H Gibson

51
beginnings

I want to bury myself like Alice

Meg and Adrienne wrote to each other after meeting when Adrienne was at home in New Zealand for a brief holiday. Meg 'seduced Adrienne with poetry and letters over several months', sending her a poem every Tuesday. Adrienne's letter to Meg was written in reply in July 1998.

PRIVATE COLLECTION

'98 Tues. afternoon 21st July
(Knowing you will call tonight)

Too Long to Wait or "Not all the flowers here have nectar"

The sea won't stop sparkling today
you are there sparkling in each dancing diva
you are heart sparkle in me
like Alice I want to find a wee small door
in your clothing. I want to be very small
     like Alice
I want to climb right into the warm place
     between your breasts
I want to stay there for a long time
     will you let me?

Sophie Ode to Chris Brougham

Sophie Ode from Lyon and Chris Brougham from Wellington met in a youth hostel in Barcelona in 1994, and this letter was written by Sophie to Chris soon after. The 'place' is the main square in Barcelona. After corresponding and periods of living together in New Zealand and France, they separated in 1997.

COLLECTION OF CHRIS BROUGHAM

Chris, little by little I realise how precious you are for me — How precious, how agreeable was this impression of freedom I had with you. To always be myself, because I knew you would never judge me — just because I wanted you to know me as I wanted to know you ... and that's why our silences were so light ...

As I'm telling you this, I know I would be able to go on living as nothing happened between us. Just by letting time work. But would this have a sense? When, perhaps, we could build and share something together? ...

Saturday evening, I went to an elegant, very elegant party, with lots of marvellous dresses, and gentle men to make them turn — I thought it would be funny. But it was mainly boring, until the moment I forgot the general atmosphere! It's terrible, these places so full of people, and so empty of emotions!

I'll never forget the birds flying in the place.

Soon, we'll be together, Chris — Sophie.

We should seemingly break off — John Prendeville to Amelia Monaghan

Amelia Monaghan was 18 when she met John Prendeville in Wellington in 1874. Amelia's mother, however, was less than happy about their courtship so they arranged to leave letters for each other at the Wellington Public Library. The couple married some months later.

COLLECTION OF MARY POLKINGHORNE

Makara
Oct 27th 1874

My Dear Love

After thinking over the fatal words "We must part", I have come to the conclusion that it is better we should <u>seemingly</u> break off for awhile, in the meantime we are to determine and arrange how and when we are to meet. Should your mother still persist in abusing you on my account tell her we have shook hands and parted. I hope she will then be satisfied. My visits unless on business will be fewer. I dare say it may be better to break them off altogether.

Do not forget you have another father and mother. Place your trust in them. They will assuredly be your protection. Heaven will not permit that hearts united by the pure ties of mutual affection should be severed on account of another transgression. You know I am no more responsible for my sister's words or acts than for those of any other person; yet,

I dare say I shall have to bear the brunt of her follies; but it is altogether unjustifiable that your young heart should suffer in the vortex.

Under the present circumstances we must I fear take someone of your family into our confidence. This and other matters we must arrange. Our correspondence must not be preserved, I fear under present circumstances your mother would not respect your feelings so much as to leave your private apartments unsearched or spare them if found.

Do not grieve in the least it will only knit our souls if possible more closely together and teach us better than cold philosophy to love the happy union that will take place when the present strife is o'er and a calm change the angry wave of passion into a placid sea.

I am as blithe as ever and request you as you love me to be so too. Laugh and smile at all.

With fondest prayer for your peace of heart and mind.
Believe me to be now and forever
Your fond and devoted lover

John S Prenderville

Archie to Lois Little

Archie Hull was born in 1916. He courted Lois Little while he was studying at university and training to be a pilot in the Royal New Zealand Air Force. Archie wrote many love letters and sonnets to Lois until his death on a training flight in 1940. Lois writes: 'He was no doubt no ordinary New Zealand young man. He was intense and moody and extremely oversensitive. I was captivated by him up to a point ...' Archie's death gave Lois 'a feeling I must join in the war'. She trained as a physiotherapist and met her husband to be, Ludwig Bieder, a recent Austrian refugee.

MANUSCRIPTS AND ARCHIVES COLLECTION, ALEXANDER TURNBULL LIBRARY MS-PAPERS-5586-02. WITH KIND PERMISSION OF LOIS BIEDER

Wednesday May 8th 1940

Dear Lois

... Very pleased to get your letter and quite overjoyed to have it confirmed that those few hours together here had as a profound effect on you as I thought they had.

I have just fished out of a pocket a handkerchief with a trace of lipstick on it and a faint smell of your perfume. How extraordinarily potent such little things like that are in establishing a contact between us, not that there isn't one all the time now.

Your letter, even the writing, is very different from any you have written before. It reflects the moods in you that I love best of all, the ones in which you are so happy that you cannot help showing it. Moods that are an expression of all about you that is lovely, moods that lift us both to the heights and without which we cannot hope to be incurably in love. I have seen you like that before but not quite so intensely.

There have been times quite often when we cannot look at each other without feeling our hearts will burst but never so much as on Saturday & Sunday. I hate feeling incompetent darling but it is so nearly impossible to tell you in words or one letter all that I feel.

It is quite revolutionary this reaction you have got in me. I've been pouring over a chart all afternoon losing myself because I guess my mind is not so much concerned with the course I would steer to Heligoland as with the course I would like to be steering for Wellington, and all the times I've been thinking about what you are doing — having afternoon tea perhaps talking to Margaret, being admired by some one arriving home, playing with Peter and sitting in front of the fire & then I have to stop for fear my brain goes soft.

I have read your letter several times and yet I want to read it again, not so much because it is flattering to me as that it convinces me that we have both stopped swerving and are on the right track.

I shall treasure this letter always — it's quite lyrical darling. I love the way you have the gift of giving to simple words the exquisite power of suggestion and I wish you would do it more ...

To be so close to beauty was of itself the most perfect thing that I have ever known, you are so very lovely Lois and yet all your beauty of body and beauty of soul is only part, though the greatest part of the bigger thing we call our love.

Does it all sound maudlin darling, perhaps the words are but the emotions are not. If we were together again I could make you know again couldn't I? Darling keep us both feeling like this as long as you can. You are irresistible when you want to be. If only you will want hard enough ... Good night darling. Archie

Bramwell Cook to Dorothy Money

Bramwell Cook and Dorothy Money first met in Christchurch in 1926 when Dorothy was 13 and Bramwell 22. When Bramwell travelled to London in 1929 to continue his medical studies they began to correspond. They met again when Bramwell returned to New Zealand in 1931, prior to his departure to India to serve as Chief Medical Officer at the Salvation Army hospital at Anand.

Bramwell and Dorothy corresponded increasingly more often after his arrival in India. In 1932, Dorothy resolved to commit her life to missionary service and wrote Bramwell a 10-page letter about her decision. Bramwell responded immediately, inviting her to work by his side as his wife and partner in the Salvation Army.

Dorothy's response to Bramwell's marriage proposal was by letter and not by the suggested cablegram. This meant that he had to wait eight weeks for her reply. Finally, her letter arrived in Anand on Boxing Day 1932. The text of the letter is unknown, but Bramwell's response following tells it all.

Dorothy arrived in India in February 1935, only five days before her marriage to a man she knew mainly through his letters. It was, as Bramwell wrote to her shortly before their reunion, 'a venture of faith'. The marriage proved to be extremely happy and productive. The couple remained in India until 1953, and their five children were born there.

COLLECTION OF BRAMWELL COOK, SON OF BRAMWELL AND DOROTHY

Anand
Boxing Day 1932

My Darling Dorothy,

Your long awaited letter arrived — this morning. What a beautiful Xmas present!

I admire your candidness and restraint and I love you all the more for the balanced way you look at things. If there is one thing I am anxious to be careful about, it is not to rush you or force you.

I want you to decide yourself what steps you will take in the future. I know I can be happy in that your steps will be in alignment not only with your own feelings but also will be with regard to what is God's will for you.

I do love the way you look at things. I have always felt my life has been ordered by God and if you feel the same, how happy I will be. I am a very practical and earthly fellow and I want some spiritual ballast (or uplift) in my helpmate! And I felt at once in reading the letter in which you spoke of your call to service that you were the very one I needed — and the letter I received today more than reassures me. Am I counting my chickens too soon! I feel I am not, but I am quite prepared to wait til you can definitely commit yourself ...

I love you more than ever Dot. And I feel that as we interchange letters, in spite of thousands of miles of sea, our love will grow deeper and deeper. What a happy day it will be when we meet! ...

Five weeks later Bramwell received two letters from Dorothy which 'set my heart abounding'. He wrote immediately.

'These two letters have made me ever so happy. I can understand how startling, how disturbing was my proposal — and I have loved and appreciated your careful consideration. But at the same time you will realise how hungry I was for your full acceptance. And I read it in these letters ...'

66 Courtney Place

The donor of this letter to the Wairarapa Archive was unable to provide any information about Allan and Alice, the writer and recipient.

COLLECTION OF THE WAIRARAPA ARCHIVE

66 Courtney Place
1 May 1900

My own Sweet love
I hope you arrived safely.

The weather here today has been unputupable. Dearest sweetest Alice I feel miserable, without you life is not worth living. I long to see your sweet Angelic face, those languishing eyes, your lovely form sends a magnetic sensation through my heart and soul.

I am longing for a Photo by return, and hope sweet Angel you won't forget me if you do lovely Alice you will break my heart and cause my existence to be a dreary wilderness, and without the sunshine of sweet Alice I cannot be happy.

Kindly send size of finger that I may send a present of a ring in the meantime it won't be an expensive one but no matter how small the gift it will be a small remembrance from one who loves you spiritually who loves you heart and soul from one who would die for you.

Please send letters & photo to 66 Courtney Pl.

Ever Yours
till death
Allan

Ian to Fay, Johannesburg 1953

Fay Caldwell and Ian Roy met while working at the South British Insurance Company in Wellington. After a brief courtship, the company sent Ian to Kenya in 1953. Here Ian writes to Fay after arriving in Johannesburg on the way to Mombasa. Ian remained in Africa for two years and on his return they were married.

COLLECTION OF FAY ROY

Carlton Hotel, Johannesburg
31-8-53

Dear Fay,

I just called around to the South British Office and picked up my mail. I received a letter from Dad and then I saw 2 type addressed envelopes. I rushed back to the Hotel, took a drag on my cigarette to slow down the heart beat & steady the nerves, then started reading. Honey, Honey, it's dangerous writing me letters like that. I'd look silly swimming the Indian Ocean on my way back to New Zealand wouldn't I. Still to express in words how pleased I was to get them is beyond my powers. I'm sure it is enough for me to say that wherever I am, whatever the temptations as far as I'm concerned the little girl I found happiness with in Wellington is the girl I'm going to see again as soon as I can make it. I know you realise that this move of mine is for my own good and though I'd like to be with you now, fate has destined other things. As you say it's cold comfort having a photograph but by God it's better than nothing.

Now beautiful you get that coloured photograph to Mombasa with all speed. I know you think you are cute but then so do I and as you say photos never lie. Another thing you lay off this bloke Stephenson. Your letter was Murray this Murray that (that is when you weren't saying nice things to me). I'm getting jealous kid, as jealous as a bloke can be when he can't do a thing about it. Are you still my girl? I hope so, oh! how I hope.

That was a good idea of your Mum's about "Aussy" kitten but I think that when I get my leave I'll beat it back to NZ as fast as a "Rocket Ship" can get me there. I don't think I'll want to stop over in Australia. Of course this may just be a dose of Homesickness, with your clearer mind you may be able to tell.

I'm glad you got those photos of me on the ship. I know Mum will appreciate them. I don't really want a copy of the photo of all you girls if it's not so good. Frankly with due respect to all there is only one, who I am <u>extremely</u> interested in. (note underlining).

Tommy Trinders girls (if on board) weren't anything. One <u>floss</u> (definitely not a type to associate with) tired to do a line with me, God only knows what for, and I had great pleasure in telling her how keen I was on a girl back in NZ, so much that I wasn't particularly interested in speaking to young females on the boat. Needless to say she didn't bother speaking to me again and started work on some more pliable material.

I'm glad Dad is fixing up about the Ring and in his letter he let me know the date it would be ready so by now you may have it back again.

I'm afraid I've been showing off a bit lately. Both on board the ship and in Capetown the boys I've met have had a tendency to drag out Photos of their Girl friends. I couldn't let a thing like that slide so I had to show them your picture and I must admit that you are definitely the most attractive thing I've seen yet, and they say you've got brains too. What an amazing combination.

Well Fay because of all my burbling in this letter form I'll now have to write you telling all about things up to Johannesburg.

From your sentimental boy
Ian

For the last time in our single lives — Ernest Hobbs to Lily Macdonald

Ernest Hobbs wrote this letter to his fiancée, Lily Macdonald, two days before their marriage on 28 May 1913. Ernest and Lily had been courting for six years, and may have initially met through the Wellington Brethren Church that they both attended.

COLLECTION OF GEOFF TILYARD

My Very Own Darling Loving Lily

Just a few lines for probably the last time in our single lives. I hope the next time I write to you to do so as my darling little wife. Which is better than all the letters we can ever write as sweethearts.

My loving Lily it is only a matter of two days now and we will be wed after all these long years of courtship. It is hard to think that my long tramps and wet wintry nights are within a few hours of exchanging places with the blissful happiness of a dear little woman's love. Of course I know you have always loved me sweetheart but only as a lover, but the time is almost at hand when you can love me with a love that only a wife can know.

I must not say too many smoogy things old sweetheart. I will say all these again Wednesday ...

Au revoir for a little while.
I remain your loving sweetheart until Wednesday
Ernest Hobbs

it is not all honey being on the tramp | journeys

CHRISTCHURCH POSTMEN CIRCA 1900

Donald to Susan McLean

Donald McLean and Susan Strang met in 1849 and were married on 24 August 1851. About six weeks after their marriage, Donald McLean resumed his job as a government land purchase officer, leaving Susan to spend most of her time at her parents' house caring for her ailing mother. By 9 October 1851, six weeks after the wedding, Susan writes that she is pregnant — though this baby was later miscarried. On 18 October 1851, she writes to him: 'How much I wish darling that you were back ... I know dearest, that although you are away from me that your thoughts are always with me and that you share with me in all your troubles and trials.'

In March 1852, Susan is pregnant again. When Donald is not calling Susan 'Pussy', he refers to her by her second name, Douglas — the name of the expected son Susan is carrying.

MANUSCRIPTS AND ARCHIVES COLLECTION, ALEXANDER TURNBULL LIBRARY MS-PAPERS-0032-0828

Crofton N Zealand
4 April 1852
(raining hard)

You cannot conceive how anxious I am about you Douglas therefore be sure to take every possible care of yourself in my absence. I am getting very tired of being separated from you and trust it will not be very long before you either hear from me or see me. But my greatest earthly enjoyment now is to be with my own little pussy — goodbye dear. Give my love to Mamma. Tell Jessie to be a good girl, and always believe me your own affectionate Donald McLean.

Donald McLean returned to Wellington early in September 1852 and was there when their son Douglas was born on 7 November. Susan endured a painful labour and died the same day. This is one of her last letters to Donald.

MANUSCRIPTS AND ARCHIVES COLLECTION, ALEXANDER TURNBULL LIBRARY, MS-PAPERS-0032-0827

Aug 24 1852

My dearest Donald

This is the anniversary of the happy day on which I became yours ... I cannot sit up long as I do not feel well ... I am sure dearest, few others, having been married a year, are as fond of each other as we are and I trust my darling if we are long spared to live together our love will increase every year and I hope we may never have cause to regret our marriage but that we may always consider it the happiest day in our lives. I know my dearest love that I have your entire affection and I am sure it will be my own fault if I lose it. The longer I am your wife the more my affection for you increases. I have not a single wish or hope that is not connected with my dear husband ...

God bless you my own love ...
Susan D. McLean

Annie Hill to Anna Richmond

Anna Richmond was born in 1855 into the 'Richmond-Atkinson Clan' based in Nelson. Anna suffered from asthma and other illnesses but was a keen letter writer and collected a great many of the letters sent to her.

Annie Hill was a close friend of hers when both families lived in Nelson. Annie wrote this letter to Anna when she was staying with her sister in Batavia, Java in 1877. Annie had recently refused an offer of marriage. Like many female friends, Annie writes freely of her love for Anna. Women sometimes seem to have enjoyed closer relationships with their wome friends than with their suitors or husbands.

Annie Hill later married the Reverend F. W. Chatterton of Nelson.

MANUSCRIPTS AND ARCHIVES COLLECTION, ALEXANDER TURNBULL LIBRARY MS-PAPERS-77-173-10

June 5th 1877

Dear old Anna

...You know what your friendship has been to me and I trust will always be as long as we live. You know how much I love you and how I long to have your love and confidence in return; but I have wished to hear <u>you</u> express it in words, I longed to hear loving longing words from you to show me that you prized <u>my</u> friendship as much as I do yours and so this proof that you thought often of me and were anxious to hear from me, is very dear to me.

You will think it very strange and unbelieving of me to require these additional proofs of your friendship but I can't help it, it is my nature to long for demonstrative proofs of love, and so when ever you write words that prove that my love is not quite valueless to you, it makes my heart glad and burst over with love for my very dear good constant friend. I wish indeed that you were "a nice young man" even <u>minus</u> the black whiskers, how happy should I be if I could find a husband that I could love and trust in so thoroughly as I do you ...

Just over 17 hours since we parted — Brian to Heather Barker

Heather Boyd and Brian Barker met in 1969 when Heather was 14. They eloped two years later. This letter was written in 1979 when the Barkers had decided to emigrate from New Zealand to Ireland. They had sold their house, and Heather had gone ahead with their two children to Ireland leaving Brian to tidy up loose ends before he was to follow. But the sale of the house fell through, and Heather and the children returned to New Zealand several weeks later as they 'didn't want to be parted any longer'. The Barkers remain happily married in Auckland.

COLLECTION OF HEATHER BARKER

Hello Dear

It is just over 17hrs. since we parted and I miss you all so very much. In fact it took Graham about an hour on the phone last night to convince me that it would not be wise to get the next plane after you all but to sit tight for a few more weeks yet. I just hope this famous House Corp. gets A into G and let me know soon.

How was the flight? I hope the children were not too bad and that their ears didn't give them too much trouble. I hope [you] got a reasonable sleep also and saw some of the movies. I got very little sleep and froze also even though I had about 4 blankets on. I miss my nice cuddly heater the best thermostat on the market. Treat it gently and it will keep you warm all night. Touch the right switch and you're on boil all night. It is cold and very wet. I think even the weather is pining for you.

just remember not all the stars in the universe can buy my love for you or any word in the dictionary can explain the way I feel. Give the kids a cuddle. I love you very much. Hope to see you soon. Brian

Like a blind man fumbles as he starts out on his darkened world
I fumble my way through
The world's greatest love
Like the softness of the sea
I want to touch you so gently
My heart aches in a way like
The foal who is taken away
From his mother
You are not my mother
How can I describe what you are
You are my lover and my only lover
You are my friend and the greatest
Friend I could ever hope for
You are a wife that I thank God
For when you said I do
You are my companion and my
Inspiration in life

I love you very deeply not just in these words but even in a way that I myself cannot understand. A love that is extremely strong and strong in a strange way. It wants nobody to share it with me Wipe your tears away for I love you very much and the more I hurt you even though I don't mean to I hurt myself twice as much. I love you. Brian

Brent and Sally

Brent S. Hayward and Sally Louise Legg met in Auckland in 1995 at a video shoot. 'We had a common interest in a metaphysical counterculture and made a strong impression on each other,' says Brent.

Brent and Sally write psychedelic, passionate letters that are hand-delivered, as well as delivered by post, as a way of building their relationship. Brent says: 'We want to establish something else that exists outside of, as well as contributing to our verbal communication.'

COLLECTION OF BRENT S. HAYWARD AND SALLY LOUISE LEGG

DEH SEDANG
Kingdom of All the Sedang

All praise! All praise! All praise! Ministry of Foreign Affairs, 42, Boulevard Bouger, PELEI AGNA, SEDANG.

this is not a Sado-Methodist after-all but a bridge mending general chin wag of Ecstatic caring in sparkling eyes not lost in the storm but Living in the cherrynoble of the great Ice cream meltdown. what joy! what joy! what joy! what joy! Our Lady of the Beasts she is well pleased with the sound of rattles and of timbrels with the voice of flutes and the cry of wolves all bright-eyed Lions. You touch my soul with caress. Snakes hiss from your medusa hair lus Lussssssst, so it begins, Joy in Strength exercised Joy in desire, passion unites us to the feast. You were made in heaven. darling Sally,

Belly mi

XXX

All praise! All Praise! All Praise!

This is not a Sado-Methodist after-all but a bridge mending general chin wag of Ecstatic caring with sparkling eyes not Lost in the storm but Living in the cherynoble of the great Icecream meltdown.

What joy! What joy! What joy! Our lady of the Beasts she is well pleased with the sound of rattles and of timbrels with the voice of flutes and the out cry of wolves allbright-eyed Lions. You touch my soul with caress. Snakes hiss from your medusa hair dust Lussssssst. So it begins, Joy in Strength exercised Joy in desire, passion unites us to the feast. You were made in heaven darling Sally, Eurynome rose naked from chaos, she danced toward the East, she set the wind in motion, she danced toward the South, the Lightening flashed above her, she danced toward the west, she danced upon the waters, she danced toward the north, she felt the cold wind on her. She rubbed it between her hands, it became Ophion the great serpent, she danced harder she was cold, Ophion watched her, He grew hot, he wrapped himself around her limbs, they fucked, she became a dove brooding on the waves, she laid it, he coiled around it seven times out came all the things that exist

The sun and the earth

Pps my connection with you makes me more connected toward us.
Xxxxxxxxxxxxxxxxxxxxxxxxxxxxxxxxxxxxxxxxxxxxxxx
Brent S. Hayward

Ours is the God given pure love — Les Jerram to Vera

Les Jerram wrote to his wife, Vera, while he was away surveying land in 1919.

COLLECTION OF CLAIRE HADEN

Survey Camp
Sunday 7th

Dearest girl,

… I know you need me and I cannot come, but dear, I will be with you soon, and we must try and bear up a little longer. It is a supreme test for us both and some great author once said that until lovers were parted, they did not know what true love was. We have now found it beyond doubt, ours is the God given pure love, and I am very thankful, but very sad when I am away from you.

Darling girl the work here is setting me up and I am now as fit as a fiddle, I have had no dinner to-day it is now 3pm so I must get back to camp & tuck in. Soon the time will come when you will be crushed to pulp in my arms once more dearest Vera mine, so adieu.

Yours ever & ever
Les xxx hundred

Survey Camp
Sunday 7th

Dearest girl,
Your two last dear letters are beside me, and sweetheart I feel you calling me all the time, more especially at night when all is quiet in camp and I am alone with my thoughts. You naturally fill the larger part of them, and I continually make plans for you & ? but sweetheart I must finish this survey & until then I am powerless, I shall without doubt have something settled with Tommy by Xmas. He has written me saying he is very pleased with my work here, and so I will possibly be able to work something with him at Xmas when I see him.

Dear, I have just ridden 16 miles, first down to Hallams for letters & stores, then up the Motu road to Toa Toa, where I am now writing this epistle, as I still have another 3 miles

You are my life — Len Douglas

Dr Lennox Douglas wrote to Joan Reid over the 20 plus years spanning his medical school days, courtship, marriage and during his military training and war service in Egypt during World War II. He was the first New Zealand doctor killed on active service when he volunteered as senior surgeon in the evacuation of Greece. He left a family of three daughters, Catherine, Ann, and Mary the youngest who he never lived to see.

COLLECTION OF MARY SAXTON

19 August 1940
Trentham

My Own Darling

We are now about to start on the second stage of the adventure or crusade: taking the grim side it is a crusade, leaving you and the children to carry on, and being determined to wage war with the best young men in our countries against the young men of our enemies — it is all so stupid that the "wise men" of the tribes cannot evolve a better solution of the world problems — but taking the side of adventure, we are having a great experience in comradeship and the gathering of the clans for action. All men and all nations of any worth have had to fight for existence: but as it has it in "The Human Situation", though life is foul with tragedies and we can see no reason in such a scheme of things, we still inherit a clear vital spark and will to live.

Your own belief that our duty lies with each succeeding generation more than with ourselves is an important one: it is a purpose.

We can help them more by example and encouragement than by making their lives for them. I know you have the character and ability to show our children such things as loyalty to the heart's choice in people and in causes, faith in life's purpose and faith still when the purpose is obscure, appreciation of beauty in all her thousand ways, courage in adversity, perseverance through weary days, tolerance, and then too there is laughter — to laugh in defeat as well as in joy.

There is no need to be top of the class or rich or to excell at sport or be popular. But it does matter to be industrious and active and fair.

I hope it is not so very long before we are all together again to struggle on.

I am fighting for my King because the old traditions rouse me: I am fighting for my country because my country's cause is still the best cause in the world: and I am fighting for you and our children because you are my life.
I love you my darling.
Len

Hori Horama to William Colenso

Aroha, or love in its broadest sense, is the subject of many letters written to religious leaders by Māori in the 19th century. Letters of dedicated love and religious devotion were written to the missionary William Colenso by Māori living in Hawke's Bay and the Wairarapa during the period 1848 to 1850, including this letter, from Hori Horama. The collection of letters kept by Colenso also sheds light on the life and literacy of the two major local iwi, Ngāti Kahungunu and Rangitāne.

MANUSCRIPTS AND ARCHIVES COLLECTION, ALEXANDER TURNBULL LIBRARY MS-PAPERS-0031-039.
TRANSLATION STEPHEN CHRISP

18 Oketopa 1849

E koro, e Te Koreneho

Tēnā koe. He nui anō tōku aroha ki a koe, ahakoa kei konā koutou ko āu tamariki, me tōu hoa, me ōu hoa e noho tata ana ki a koe. Tēnei anō te aroha atu nei ki a koe. E tā, koi mahara mai koe kāhore ōku aroha atu. Tēnei ahau kai te aroha tonu atu. Tēnei, e kore e mahue te aroha.

E koro, kāhore āku kōrero pēnā. Ko tāku anō ia, he aroha anake atu ki a koe, kia Mata, ki ngā tamariki. Ehara i te aroha tinana, otirā ko te aroha whakawairua. Kei [te?] mahara tonu ahau ki ngā minita katoa, ki a Pīhopa hoki. E mahara tonu ki nga tāngata katoa.

E koro, terā anō mātou e haere atu. Tēnei he mate nōku i noho ai. Pēnei pea, ka kite tāua. E tā, māu e tuhia mai ki a mātau. I au ētahi o nga kupu o te pukapuka nei, ko ētahi reta emātau ana i au, ko ētahi kāore koia nei ahau e kī atu nei ki a koe.

Heoi anō, ka mutu.
Nāku, nā tōu hoa aroha
Nā Hōri Hōrama

18 October 1849

My elder, Mr. Colenso,

Greetings. My love for you is great indeed, although you are there with your children, your wife and your other friends that live in your neighbourhood. I love you. Friend, please don't think that I have no love for you. I love you. My love will not cease.

My elder, I would never say that. My [words] are about sending my love to you, to Mata, and to the children. It is not physical love, but rather spiritual love. I am also mindful of all of the other Ministers, and the Bishop. I am mindful of all the people.

My elder, we are leaving this place. I have remained here because of my illness. Perhaps we shall see each other. Friend, please write to us. I can follow some of the words in this letter, because I know some of the letters. However, there are some letters that I don't know. That is why I say this to you.

I shall finish here.
From your loving friend,
Hōri Hōrama

journeys

If I were to cease to love you I would cease to be happy
— Thomas King

Thomas King was devoted to his wife, Mary, and wrote to her ardently and prolifically during their occasional separations. In 1860 their farmhouse was burnt to the ground during the Taranaki War, and this letter was written when Mary and the children had to take temporary refuge in Nelson with other settlers. The King family returned to Taranaki after the war, and Thomas became the first manager of the New Plymouth branch of the Bank of New Zealand. He and Mary had several children including Frederick Truby King who went on to found the Plunket Society.

MANUSCRIPTS AND ARCHIVES COLLECTION, ALEXANDER TURNBULL LIBRARY MS-PAPERS 5641-03

6 June 1860

... It is hard to find anything to say in such a barren place as this without speaking of myself and of my love for you darling. I try to occupy my thoughts in various subjects for the contemplation of your absence is the most painful one to bear ... I think few are as much attached my Polly as you and I. I have no ambitions and I love wealth only as it will contribute to your comfort and relieve you from the constant labour you have been compelled to endure for so many years. Had this war not commenced we might soon have looked forward to great changes in our mode of life, as it is we are separated and have to endure apart greater troubles than we are called upon to encounter together ...

I am not ashamed my darling to tell you how I love you. How in the lone nights I feel the blood coursing through my veins when your image rises before me. If I were to cease to love you I would cease to be happy. For me no other woman is fair, and the remembrance of your embraces tells me of the bliss I am deprived of in my darling wife's absence.

Next month love fourteen years will have passed away since you called me to your arms from Wellington, and my Polly at forty-two will be dearer and lovelier to me than she was when I called the blushes into her cheeks in the coldroom at the Henui. I can never forget the passages of our early life — they are associated with all the happiness I have known but one fond kiss one sweet embrace will be dearer than all the ministries of the past ...

> *I want ... to get over the 'preliminaries' and live together a little* — Katherine Mansfield to Leslie Beauchamp
>
> *Katherine Mansfield was passionately fond of her only brother and youngest sibling, Leslie (Chummie) Beauchamp. Leslie travelled to England in 1915 to enlist as a soldier, and spent his last leave with Katherine in London before travelling to France in September. Two weeks later he was killed in a hand-grenade accident. This is Katherine's last letter to Leslie before his death.*
>
> MANUSCRIPTS AND ARCHIVES COLLECTION, ALEXANDER TURNBULL LIBRARY
> MS-PAPERS-2413

Dearest,

I have an odd moment to spare & I'll use it in sending you a line — Ever since last Sunday you are close in my thoughts. It meant a tremendous lot, seeing you and being with you again and I was so frightfully proud of you — you know that — but I like saying it. But the worst of it is I want always to be far <u>more</u> with you and for a long enough time for us to get over the 'preliminaries' and live together a little ...

Do you know a day when your heart feels much too big? Today if I see a flag or a little child or an old beggar my heart expands and I would cry for joy. Very absurd — I'm 26. You know — this is not a letter. It is only my arms round you for a quick minute.

Love Katie

SELFRIDGE & CO. LTD.
OXFORD STREET,
LONDON — W.

The Lounge, Reading and Writing Rooms, [25

Wednesday 19

Dearest,

I have an odd moment spare & I'll use it in sending you a line — Ever since

Joe to Zane

Joe Collins wrote this letter to his 10-year-old son, Zane, in June 1996 while he was working in Malaysia on a helicopter-logging project. In December of that year Joe was killed in a helicopter crash. This letter was contributed by Marion Day, Joe's partner and Zane's mother.

Marion writes: 'Ironically, many poems and letters Joe wrote to Zane reflected that he would not be here physically for Zane but very much in spirit.'

COLLECTION OF MARION DAY

To a special boy called Zane Collins

Hello again Zane my boy. I'm writing to you from a long way from home to tell you that you are always on my mind and in my thoughts.

You must wonder sometimes if I still think of you and love you, as I am away from you so much. I hope that one day soon I will not have to leave you and that I can be with you all the time.

You have always been my number one and have made me very proud of you many times. When you have won I have been proud, when you have lost but still try I am even more proud of you.

Your life in future will be like that, many times you will have wins, and many times you will have losses but you must not get bitter and let those times drag you down.

If you have to, get off and push yourself over the finish line just like you did in Australia. You made everyone so proud that you were in their N.Z. team, and that you didn't just give up and blame someone else.

If you are a good leader in a team you must encourage all of your team-mates, even the dumb ones. If you are a true leader and praise them often they will try harder to please you and your team will get better and stronger.

The coaches will be watching you over how you practise, are you always late, or on time, do you have clean gear, do you take practice seriously or do you not try to do as much as you can? Some players can be great, but they are not leaders because of these things.

At school I know it's very hard to concentrate on subjects you are not very good at. I am really pleased that you can read so well and enjoy your goose-bump stories so much. Reading is real important and so is writing which I know you are having trouble with. You must keep trying and not give up the race. Your good reading will help you to know how to write good stories and how to make each sentence build up your story until it is complete. Perhaps you need to think first about your subject, write down in a single word each topic you want to mention in the order you want and then begin. Pretty soon you will get it, keep it as neat as you can and you will know that it is good and will feel really happy about it.

Well my man, I had better go now, so don't forget, Dad loves you heaps even though I'm far away. I know you will always try your best, look after Mum as she loves you just as much. Goodbye boy.

Love from Dad xxx
4th June 1996

[Birthday scoldings — Mary Caroline Taylor to Mary

This is one of a series of loving yet admonishing 'birthday letters' from Mary Caroline Taylor to her daughter Mary on her 11th birthday in 1846. Mary Caroline was evidently a strong disciplinarian! Though they were both resident at the Missionary House at Putiki, it was customary for Mary Caroline to give her daughter a letter every birthday. Mary Caroline Taylor was the wife of the missionary Richard Taylor who settled in Wanganui in 1843 and played an important role in 'keeping the peace' in the Wanganui district. Daughter Mary went on to marry Lieutenant Spencer Medley. Also in Posted Love is one of Spencer's letters to Mary when they were courting (see page 30).

COLLECTION OF THE WANGANUI HISTORICAL SOCIETY, WANGANUI REGIONAL MUSEUM

July 8th 1846

My dear Mary

I am disappointed your dear Papa has not been able to return in time to unite with me in wishing you many happy returns of your birthday, you have now attained the age of 11 years and my dear little girl I wish I could say I think you possess the wisdom suitable to your age.

Do not be so soon led away and forget what you know to be your duty; our blessed Saviour has left us many blessed promises and admonitions; among the rest one I am particularly fond of namely 'Love one another; and do unto other as you would they should (under similar circumstances) do unto you', I have noticed of late an inclination to forget this blessed precept; and my beloved girl you would not willingly grieve the fond heart of your affectionate Parents; much of our future happiness depends upon our beloved children; should we see you all growing up in the fear of the Lord how happy will our old age be ...

You will perhaps think this a very serious letter but my dear child, I love you so much that I could not bear to see you grow up careless, and not remind you of the way of life, when you have a leisure hour write to me but not to day, as your time will be doubtless fully engaged and I love to see you happy and merry also; accept my fond love, and believe me your ever affectionate Mamma.

I hope you will find the little box of needles useful I fear some of them are very rusty.

'A' to 'P' — 20th-century email

Contemporary romances are often nurtured by email. 'A' and 'P' currently conduct a long-distance relationship between different cities within New Zealand.

COLLECTION OF ANN WOOLLIAMS

Subject: Re: let me count the ways …
Date: Mon, 14 Dec 1998 09:30:33+1300

where is my man
the one for me alone?
…while i was young
i first looked for?
and year by year
i searched
everywhere i knew?

i want this man —
familiar and like a stranger,
who comes so close;
quiet kisses, gentle caresses,
silent at the point of
passionate infinity …
forever out of reach

… ?
it is you isn't it?
i truly hope so!
i want you for my life, my love …
you have taken my heart;
(who told you to?)
seduced my mind …
intrigued and mesmorized me;
you are a blinding light

and forever
you will hear me call;
through the ages,
eons and eternity;
my true love

Chris Kraus — I Love Dick

This letter is one of a series by Chris Kraus, a writer who grew up in New Zealand and currently lives in Los Angeles. The letters were actually written and sent, and then compiled in a book entitled I Love Dick. *Described as an act of performative philosophy,* I Love Dick *achieved some notoriety when the recipient, named in the book only as 'Dick', unsuccessfully tried to block publication.*

I LOVE DICK PUBLISHED BY SEMIOTEXTE, USA

Dear Dick,

I want to write to you about schizophrenia even though I haven't got a wooden leg to stand on in relation to this subject, having never studied it or experienced it first hand. But I'm using you to create a certain schizophrenic atmosphere, OR, love is schizophrenia, OR, I felt a schizophrenic trigger in our confluence of interests — who's crazier than who? Schizophrenia's a state that I've been drawn to like a faghag since age 16. For years I was the best friend, confidante, of schizophrenics. I lived through them, they talked to me. In New Zealand and New York, Ruffo, Brian, Erje and Michelle, Liza, Debbe, Dan, were conduits for getting closer. But since these friendships always end with disappearances, guns and thefts and threats, by the time we met I'd given up. When I asked you if you'd been to school you acted like I'd asked you if you still liked fucking pigs. "Of course I've been to school." After all, your current job depends on it. But I could tell from all the footnotes in your writing that you hadn't. You like books too much and think they are your friends. One book leads you to the next like serial monogamy. Dear Dick, I've never been to school but every time I go into a library I get a rush like sex or acid when you're starting to get off. My brain gets creamy with associative thought. Here are some notes I made about schizophrenia:

1. Schizophrenia consists of placing the word "therefore" between two non-sequiters. Driving up to Bishop last week I had two beliefs: I wouldn't get a speeding ticket; I will die within the next five years. I didn't get a speeding ticket, therefore — (When your head's exploding with ideas, you have to find a reason. therefore, scholarship and research are forms of schizophrenia. If reality's unbearable and you don't want to give up you have to understand the patterns. "Schizophrenia," Geza Roheim wrote, "is the magical psychosis." A search for proof. An orgy of coincidences.) Two hours ago I took a break from writing this to take a walk before the sun went down. I had an urge to play Willie Nelson's Crazy on the Red Hot Country CD before going out, but didn't. When I turned the bend on 49th Terrace, my usual walk, Crazy, sung by Patsy Cline, was pouring, I mean POURING, out the windows of a house. I leaned back against a fence and watched the house lift off. An operatic, cinematic moment, everything locked into a single frame that gets you high. Oh Dick, I want to be an intellectual like you.

2. Do you remember that night in February at your house while you were making dinner, I told you how I'd become a vegetarian? I was at a dinner at Felix Guattari's loft in Paris with my husband, Sylvere Lotringer. The Berlin Wall had just come down. He, Felix, Tony Negri and Francois Pain, one of Felix's younger followers, were planning a TV panel show about the "future of the left." Sylvere would moderate a live discussion between Negri and Felix and the German playwright Heiner Mueller. They needed one more speaker. It seemed strange that people would be interested in any conversation between such a homogenous crew: four straight white European men in their 50s, all divorced and now with childless younger women in their early 30s. Sometimes coincidence is just depressingly inevitable. No matter what these four men say, it's like they've already said it. If we want reality to change, then why not change it? Oh Dick, deep down I feel that you're utopian too? "What about Christa Wolf?" I asked. (At that moment she was founding a neo-socialist party in Germany.) And all Felix's guests — the culturally important jowelly men, their Parisianally-groomed, mute younger wives, just sat and stared. Finally the communist philosopher Negri graciously replied, "Christa Wolf is not an intellectual." I suddenly became aware of dinner: a bleeding roast, prepared that afternoon by the bonne femme, floating at the center of the table.

3. Last winter when I fell in love with you and left Sylvere and moved alone up to the country, I found the second story that I'd ever written, 20 years ago in Wellington. It was written in the third person, the

person most girls use when they want to talk abut themselves but don't think anyone will listen. "Sunday afternoon, again, again," it led off. "The possibilities are not endless." Names and actual events were carefully omitted, but it describes the heartbreak and abandonment I'd felt after spending Christmas Eve with the actor Ian McIvey. I met Ian at a late-night party at the BLERTA house on Aro Street. BLERTA was a travelling rock & roll roadshow commune — a bunch of guys and friends and wives. They toured around the country in an old bus painted with cartoons by Ruffo. I was the only girl who'd showed up at this party on her own, the only journalist, non-hippie, the only person under 21, all serious disadvantages, so I was incredibly flattered when Ian hung around the edges of the chair near me. Around 3, we staggered up the road to my place for a fuck. "Aro" Street means "love" in Maori. Words left us the minute that we left the party. We were just two people walking up the street outside our bodies. Both of us were pretty drunk, and there was no way of making that transition to sex from conversation, but anyway we tried. We took our clothes off. At first Ian couldn't get It up, this pissed him off, and when he finally did he fucked me like a robot. He weighed a lot, the bed was old and squishy. I wanted him to kiss me. He turned away, passed out, I may've cried. At 8, he got up without a word and put his clothes on. "This must be the most sordid Christmas that I've spent in my whole life," the Catholic Ian mumbled, leaving. Six weeks later Douglas Weir, a TV drama produced by New Zealand's second channel, aired. The hero Douglas Weir was played with subtlety, brilliance and conviction ... by Ian McIvey. Sitting up that night at the typewriter in my bedroom where we'd fucked, writing a review for the Wellington Evening Post, I felt like Faye Dunaway being slapped by Jack Nicholson in Chinatown. I was a journalist ... a girl ... a journalist ... a girl. Hatred and humiliation gathered, soared out from my chest into my throat, as I wrote ten paragraphs in praise of Ian McIvey. That year he won Best Actor. This incident congealed into a philosophy: Art supersedes what's personal. It's a philosophy that serves patriarchy well and I followed it more or less for 20 years. That is: until I met you

love,
Chris

Mac to Nancy

Not all love letters are inspired and composed during physical separation. Angus McDonald wrote this letter to his wife, Nancy, in 1940, as he watched her with their new baby. It is one of some 650 letters he wrote to her during their marriage. Their daughter Christina writes: 'It was not an easy marriage, with their first son having spina bifida, but they rarely complained.'

COLLECTION OF CHRISTINA SMITH

1940

Nancy dearest,

To sit here and watch you and Jim gives me the loveliest feeling of pride and happiness. You are both beautiful — in the dear interest you show in one another and then of course I humbly tell myself that I'm a very lucky man to have you two. I just can't describe the lilting gladness that surges through me and often brings suspicions of tears to my eyes.

You must never think I'm unthinking! It's all in me. And even though I do not demonstrate — I assure you that if my tongue went haywire — you'd be overwhelmed with flattery and emotion.

Just a little note from Mac — inspired by watching your dear beloved actions with the babe; your smiles at him, your praise to him. And oh everything about you. Nancy I love you!

Your Mac

Nanny. I love you!
Your Mac.

> ### Dorothy to Douglas Gibbs
>
> Douglas and Dorothy Gibbs met and married in New Zealand and travelled to England during World War II. Douglas went ahead first and Dorothy wrote this note to Douglas just prior to his departure in 1939.
>
> Their son Peter Gibbs writes of their marriage: 'It was not all plain sailing, but they both weathered it well.'
>
> COLLECTION OF PETER GIBBS

Tuesday
10.45 am

My darling

I hate writing letters in a hurry especially letters that mean anything & this one means, I suppose, my whole existence. You go dear protected by so much love. I know I'm not alone in the feeling of loss at your absence but it's the deepest feeling I've ever had.

We've had such a happy five and a half years and please God we shall have more. Dear dearest thank you for those years. With no one else would I have had the lasting happiness I have had with you — I suppose because after all we have been companions. You must not worry about us, we shall carry on till you come to us. Oh happy day! When you read this think of the little horse-shoe & who is in bed below it, loving, oh loving you so much.

For ever
Your Dorothy

Frilly feet

Colonel William Lyon, Commander of the Waikato Militia, and his wife, Sophie, lived in Auckland during the 1860s and 1870s. During the New Zealand Land Wars they were separated for lengthy periods. William wrote often to Sophie during his absences, showing his affection and concern by drawing pictures of her and aspects of her dress. He writes at length about the latest fashions and the clothes that he has bought for her.

MANUSCRIPTS AND ARCHIVES COLLECTION, ALEXANDER TURNBULL LIBRARY MS-PAPERS-3947-07

Auckland
10 December 1875

My darling pet

I came back from the Thames yesterday but was most particularly unfortunate in the weather. I leave for Tauranga today (weather permitting) it has done nothing but rain for the last 48 hours, so it is just as bad here as at Wellington. I hope to be back by Xmas. Mrs McLaughlin will send your hat ... I hope you will like it, also stand up collar ...

Dr Carteril goes tomorrow by the Wellington SS to Wellington so have given him the boots to take charge of — I hope you will like them, you are now well set up. I hope the stronger shoes will fit my darling <u>frilly</u> feet, and you must not forget the <u>stripe silk stockings</u>, to show off your <u>charming leg</u> of which I am so proud and which always make me so naughty to look at, and <u>stroke</u>.

Kiss the children ...
In loving
Willie

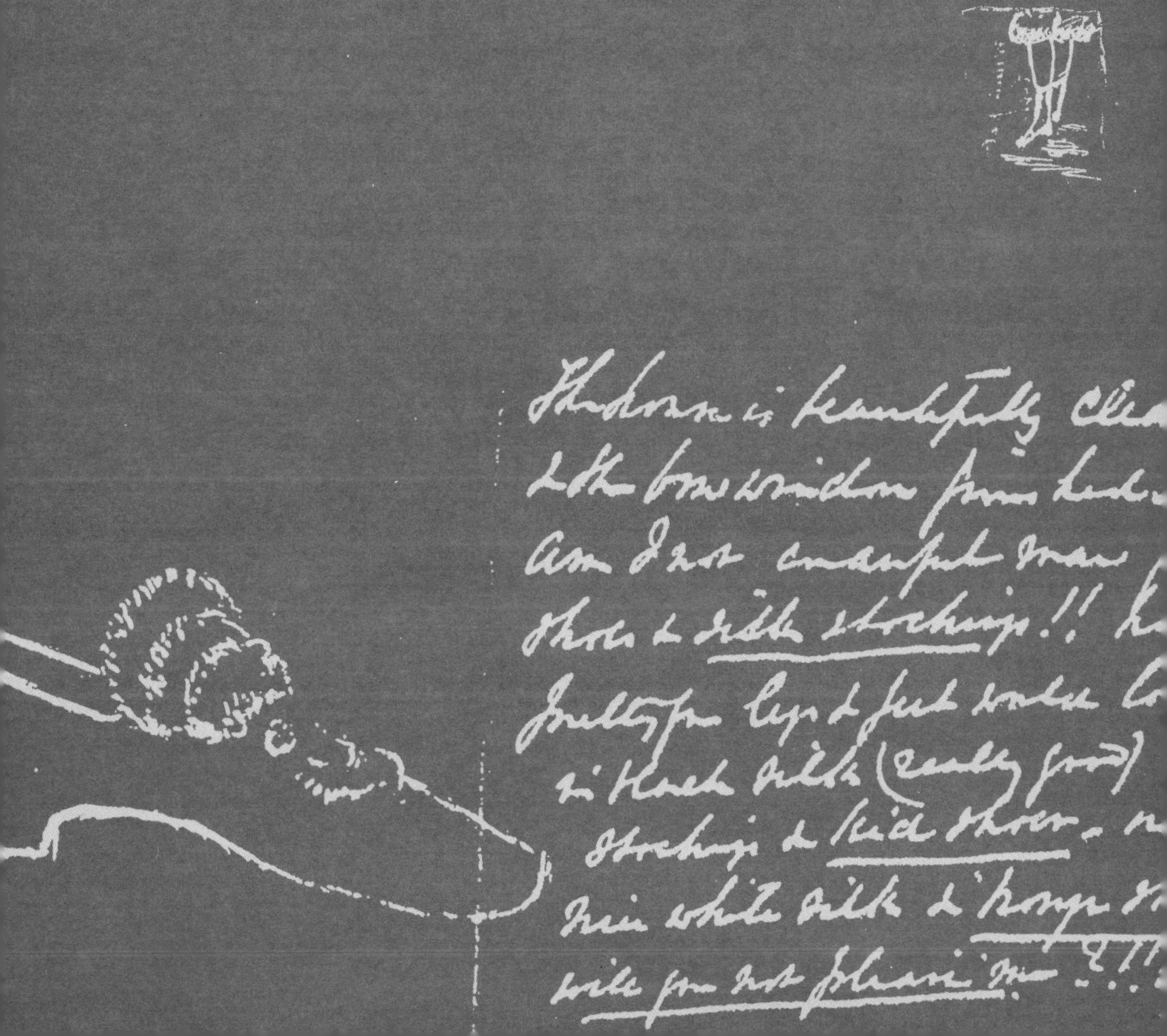
The house is beautifully clean
shoes & silk stockings!!
in black silk (really good)
stockings & kid shoes
in white silk &
will you not believe me

On the tramp — James to Harriet Crooks

James and Harriet Crooks emigrated to New Zealand from Scotland and settled in Petone. Between 1885 and 1888, James was itinerant, travelling around the North Island picking up work here and there, and sending money home to Harriet and their sons whenever he was able.

In his letter of marriage proposal to Harriet (see page 48), James Crooks had written: 'Consider it carefully over before you make your mind up, as it is for eternity not only for this life but for the life to come also — as true love can never die — but the more it is tried the purer it becomes.' It was just as well. James' later letters, of which this is one, reflect his lack of success, frequent illness and depression at not being able to provide for his family. By 1888, Harriet had become pregnant again, but James was unable to return for several months, and their situation must have seemed bleak. No further correspondence has survived. James died in Upper Hutt on 21 March 1889 at the age of 35, just a year after his last recorded trek.

MANUSCRIPTS AND ARCHIVES COLLECTION, ALEXANDER TURNBULL LIBRARY MS-PAPERS-6243

Patea
23 March 1888

My own dear Lass

I am unfortunate again in not being able to send you money as I expected as I have been able just to earn what has paid for my bed and one or two meals a day since I left Wanganui, and to-night I start on the road back again to Petone. What a long walk over 200 miles the shortest way I can go. but as I have worked that way up I must take a longer & more round about way in order to make some money — which means about 300 miles — unless I take Foxton way which is over 100 miles from here but I don't expect to be home under a fortnight or three weeks, but I'll try my very best to make what I can for you and the boys. This is a dreadfull place, today I have made 2/- yesterday 3/- the day before 3/6. and some days I have only made 1/6. So you see old love it is not all honey being on the tramp by any means ...

Now old Love how are the boys and yourself. I hope you are all well. The job I expected to get when I came here was taken a week before I arrived as I was too late — and I wish I had never come but had turned back from Wanganui when I got that length, but it is too late to grumble now. I do wish I was at home again. This is dreadfull this going on and you may be sure that I'll be home as soon as I can get, to see that 'man and the dog' and your own dear self, as well as the boys. Kiss them for me and give them my love ...

And with God's help I'll soon be home again
Yours Ever till death
Jim

Ern to Jenny Beaglehole

David Ernest (Ern) Beaglehole wrote to his wife, Jane (Jenny), every wedding anniversary. Ernest and Jenny married on 23 July 1895 and lived in Wellington.

Grandson Tim Beaglehole writes: 'David Ernest Beaglehole was a serious-minded young man who found in literature the key to that ideal of self-improvement central to the Methodist teaching of his youth.' The deep passion that can be read in his letters to Jenny is in stark contrast to the 'serious-minded young man' that his family remember him to be.

COLLECTION OF TIM BEAGLEHOLE

July 23rd 1920

Dear Mother

Isn't it wonderful? Or, can it be possible — twenty five years — it's been a wonderful time. And this morning I come to you to bring you afresh my love, my devotion, my worship, more intense than ever from the comradeship of the years. This seems to have been the philosophy of it all:

'Dear love', he said, that morning long ago,
'Where Life may lead the wisest cannot know,
or through what changing weather.
If I could choose, no cloud should dim the sky.'
She smiled, 'What matter where the road maybe so we two walk together.'

'So we two walk together.' And that's been the summing up of it all, and the beauty of it, and the glory of it. This is my supreme joy this anniversary day, this, <u>that we have walked together</u>. Darling, I bless whatever Gods there be for all the joy and happiness — the deep, assuring triumphant happiness — you have brought to me, and of which I am conscious so tremendously this morning.

Oh I cannot express what is welling up in my heart but when I recall that day twenty five years ago when our two lives joined and we took up our fellowship of love and life, and think of what the years have brought us. I cannot understand how it is that such wonderful joy should have come to me. Oh but I could shout for the splendour of it — you wonderful woman, what adorable love and sweetness has been yours. My heart sings I love you, I love you, I love you ...

Your husband *Your husband*
E
E

99
journeys

Lumpy porridge

Mrs C. P. Pleasants writes of this letter: 'My father wrote to my mother when she was holidaying in Wellington in 1918. The original of this letter has become a prized possession in our family.'

COLLECTION OF PLEASANTS FAMILY

My darling little woman,

Just how long do you m[ean]
Not more than a week I ho[pe]
That to try and live witho[ut you]
Seems to be a silly sor[t]
You start in the morni[ng]
The porridge gets in lu[mps]

Burnside
Halcombe
27th July 1918

My darling little woman

Just how long do you intend to be away.
Not more than a week I hope, I'd like to say.
That to try and live without one's loving wife
Seems to be a silly senseless kind of life.
You start in the morning by lighting the fire
The porridge gets in lumps which raises your ire.
The chops get all burnt for the trouble began
By forgetting the fat, they stuck to the pan.
To clean the pan, oh! what an awful set out
I scrubbed, I scraped but the dirt could not get out.
For dinner the spuds, well they could not compare
With those that you cook, for the salt was not there.
For a pudding I tried to make one with rice
It turned out a failure 'twas not at all nice
For tea I sat down to a cheerless array
A spread for one only the rest all away,
Save Kitty-cat and Ginger, look out there, damn!
While my back was just turned they collered the ham.
The tea-things all washed up I retired to write
I just got well started when out goes the light
No oil in the lamp, of that you may be sure
So don't be long darling I can't endure more
I'll meet you next Friday I hope you are well.
Till then 'au revoir' from you loving boy Lel

God's will be done — Thomas to Grace Hirst

Thomas and Grace Hirst and their five children emigrated to New Zealand in 1851. The family farmed and traded in Taranaki for 10 years before returning to England in late 1860 when martial law was declared during the New Zealand Land Wars.

When the Hirsts left England again to return to New Zealand in September 1861, their ship the William Brown caught fire off the coast of Madeira, and the family was rescued and taken back to England. Thomas returned to New Zealand on another ship immediately, but Grace had been very distressed at the ordeal on the William Brown and remained in England until late 1862. Thomas had hoped up until the last minute that she might join him on the passage and his letters betray his love for her and his sorrow at their separation.

MANUSCRIPTS AND ARCHIVES COLLECTION, ALEXANDER TURNBULL LIBRARY
MS-PAPERS-0996

Nov 29th 1861

The contemplated meeting afforded me the most exquisite feeling I ever experienced. I do not write thus to blame you nor to give you pain — but you know I have often poured out my feelings to your ever loving heart it always did me good — it does me good to write thus ... To me you have ever been as my Guardian angel — if I have been good and useful and a blessing I owe you much for it. I do not deserve the blessedness of your society — it has been the great happiness of my married life — God has blessed me in and through you ...

Dec 1st

The ship is now 2.50 pm under weigh with a fair Wind — It is God's will that you do not now join me ... Great as this disappointment is to me — yet I can say God's will be done — and that without repining —

I have been this day in such a fever of excitement about seeing you ... I am glad it is over. I am not sorry that I have written such passionate letters to you — for I believe they will not harm you — but one thing I will say they were the genuine feelings of my heart.

Into the sea

Private Thomas Hughes was on his way to World War I in September 1914 when he wrote a letter to his wife, placed it in a bottle and threw it into the English Channel. He died 12 days later on the French Front. It was 85 years before his message was discovered by an English fisherman, Steve Gowan. Thomas' wife and daughter had emigrated to New Zealand some years after Thomas' death, and on discovery of the letter in a bottle Steve Gowan was brought out to New Zealand to present the letter to Thomas' daughter, Emily Crowhurst.[14]

COLLECTION OF EMILY CROWHURST. A COPY IS HELD AT THE NATIONAL LIBRARY OF NEW ZEALAND

(covering note)

Sir or Madam, Youth or Maid

Would you kindly forward enclosed letter and earn the blessing of a poor British soldier, on his way to the front this 9th day of September 1914.

Signed

Pte T. Hughes

2nd Durham Light Infantry

3rd Army Corps

Expeditionary Force

September 8/9th, 1914

Dear Wife

I am writing this note on this boat and dropping it into the sea just to see if it will reach you. If it does, sign this envelope on the right hand bottom corner where it says receipt. Put the date and hour of receipt and your name where it says signature and look after it well.

Ta ta sweet, for the present

Your Hubby

XX

Friday

Endawo
? Tempsig
silverthorn

My dearest Jack;
This is just a little
hoping you reached your d
safe and sound.
I have been thinking of y
you left, and of the little
intended making before
and how it petered out
wanted to wish you all the
in the world;   and to th

Lilian to Jack Elworthy

This letter was written by Lilian Elworthy to her husband, Jack. Their daughter, Jo, writes: 'I found it still folded, and very creased, in his paybook, where he had carried it with him throughout the war. He was captured on Crete, and was a prisoner in Germany until 1945. He came back to New Zealand in 1947.

'My parents, like a lot of Kiwi parents, were never very demonstrative of affection towards each other, so for me it was lovely to see in this letter my mother's love for my father.'

COLLECTION OF JO, JULIET AND JOHN ELWORTHY

>   Friday
>   "Bendavis"
>   Pempsey Street
>   Silverstream

My dearest Jack

This is just a little note hoping you reached your destination safe and sound.

I have been thinking of you since you left, and of the little speech I intended making before you went and how it petered out. I wanted to wish you all the luck in the world; and to thank you for all the work you did about the place before you left to make things easier for me: I do appreciate everything so much; and want you to know, that wherever you go, my thoughts and fondest love go with you: I know my days will contain an empty spot, until you come home again; and so dear one, take extra special care of yourself won't you.

I haven't been able to settle to work today; but have spent more than a few moments chasing the birds off the front lawn; I think however, they have left us some seed, as there are quite a lot of tufts of young grass visible. The proofs of the photographs came this afternoon; I am a bit disappointed in them; the ones of you alone are not a bit like you; you look about fifty; so I shall not get any taken off; but the others are not so bad; Estry's hands are moving in two of them: the ones with you holding him, are I think, the best; however, I won't look at them any more tonight, and maybe my verdict will be different tomorrow.

Ronnie came down this afternoon, and asked if she could go walking with us, as she was so fed up; I can't see her staying at Rangimarie much longer.

Miss Adams came this morning and bought me some flowers; and was very sweet; she said her Mother was so pleased you went along to see her, and thought how handsome you looked.

Estry has been a very good boy today; and kept looking over to your place this morning; raising his eyebrows at the absence of 'whiskers'. I tried to explain matters to him as well as I could, but I'm sure he missed pulling your hair, and your nose.

I don't know if you wanted any of the snaps you developed, darling but am enclosing two; if you want more you can let me know. Also if you have time to write dear will you let me have your cousin's address; and the address to write you when you leave N.Z.; I think it is c/- G.P.O.

Have no more 'news' at the moment, so will close, sending you all my fondest love and thoughts; and may it be but a little while before you are home with us again. Estry sends his love to old whiskers.

Cheerio for now Sweetheart
Your ever loving Wife
Lilian XXXXXxx

this bare memory that you were here

Bob, Bil and Mery

Bob, the writer of this letter, is virtually illiterate, but if you persevere with this letter his words and message become more legible. The recipient, 'Mery', a 'maiden aunt', died recently, but had made no mention of either 'Bil' or Bob to her family, so we can only speculate on the relationship between Bob and 'Mery'. The date of the letter and the reference to the 'Turks' suggest that Bob was writing after serving at Gallipoli.

PRIVATE COLLECTION

Camp
Feb 28 1916

Dear Mery,

i don no if u wil like to git a letr from me — u sed if i went 4 a solgr u wood av no think mor 2 do wiv me an u wood av bil and e never wos no good an as gorn an dyd of feavr so wot bout me now —

bil never was no good an es went out wiv feavr.

u sed u av no think 2 do if i went 4 a soldr but bil es gorn an dyd of fevr an no turk stuk him lik a turk stuk me in a plas i carnt tork orf, cors it luk lik i run a way wich it wur not Mery ony it wurnt much 2 luk at an i nevvr went 2 no doktor not i lik bil an i stuk the Turk.

u sed you wood av no think 2 do wiv me if I went 4 solgr 4 i mite git wondid an it is ony a little wond an don mattr cors its in a plas tht don mattr but bil e dyd of feavr in orspital now bil's dyd an gorn, pore bil e dyd of fever. u sed u wood av no think 2 du wiv me if i went for a solgr ?? of feavr like bil pore bil it wos ony a littel prog i got so i fort u wood av me now an i didn get no woodn leg an no woodn arm and no blooin glars i, ony a littel prog wear it don mattr only u mite av found it won day so i tole you now.

Now u now bils dyd of feavr will u av me if i don get no wood leg nor no think an don git wondid egsept wear it don mattr Mery.

Yours
Bob

III endings

Charles Perrin, on death

Charles Perrin courted Sophia Bollen in October and November 1855 in New Town, England. Once married, the couple emigrated to New Zealand from Dorset in 1874, sailing on the Berar. Little is known about their marriage. Despite Charles' early obsession with death and contemplation of suicide, he lived until 1923 when he must have been nearly 90.

MANUSCRIPTS AND ARCHIVES COLLECTION, ALEXANDER TURNBULL LIBRARY
MS-PAPERS-2579-02.

Hatcham New Town
November 20th 1855

My Dearest Sophia

Although I have seen you so lately, I thought I should like to write to you, you cannot think what a pleasure it is to me to write to you, it is next in happiness to seeing you, I hope you are not low spirited, for I am not, I feel better now than I have done before after an hollowday for some time past. this time it was spent more in accordance with my own taste, there was no dancing and wromping, wich I do not like, it allways gives me the headace and makes me low spirited the next day, this time it was spent as it ought to be spent, in a quiet harmless way.

I shall be glad when Sunday comes again to see you, I should like to have an hour alone with you, to talk over what is to be done. I did not like to hear you talk as you did about me going away, seeing as you must, that it is all for your good, as well as it is for mine, with me it seem the road to happiness with you it seem all dark and feerfull what is there in it you do not like are you afraid that the Allmighty is not sufficiant to keep me from dangers on the sea as well as on land you cannot think that.

If it is his will that I should die on the sea or in a forein land, I am willing to submit to his call, My Dearest think of this, To live is Christ, but to die is great gain, If you felt this as strongly as I do, you would not think Death such a terrible thing, or wish anybody back again into this world, and again I am not going to fight, I am going in a good cause, one that you ought to feel proude to see me in. I shall be in good company, and have good exampels set before me. and I hope I shall do nothing to disgrace the flag under wich I sail.

What is a year or two if it is repaid with a life time of happiness, the time will soon fly away, and then I shall return to home and you, with the world's prize in my pocket, wich I see no chance of obtaining at home, you know if we want happiness we must seek it, and I do not care how dearley I pay for it if I can bear with the reefs of the bargan, and shair it with you, for My Dearest Girl I shall never love another, I could go away tonight and be happy, if I knew you would be happy, there will allways be a home for you when ever you like to come, wich is a great pleasure for me to know.

But I shall not go before the opening of the year, Dearest if you wish to see me happy give me your best wishes and bid me go, the thoughts of you will cheer me on all through the prize?

Oh, how sweet will my evenings be
While laying on the gentle heaving sea
And watching the stars as they twinkle above
Thinking of home and youth's first love

Oh My Dearest these thoughts make me wish I was there far, far away hidden from all human eyes where none but God can see me then I shall have a closer walk with God, what is better than sollowtude to soften and purefy the mind, but now Dearest I must conclude with kindest love to you, and believe me to remain your ever Loveing and faithfull

Charley

P.S I heartley thank you for writing your name on my card I wish I had seen it last night so that I could have kissed you and thanked you for it then but accept my thanks and you shall never want while I have a penny left. Good night Dearest and may God bless us both is the wish of your Charley.

(2) M 20 Nov

as you must, that it is al[l]
as well as it is for mine,
seem the road to happi[ness]
seem all dark an[d] fe[arful]
are in it you do not li[ke]
... that the Almighty
[w]ant to keep me from
the sea as well as on [land]
think that If it is hi[s]
...
own land, I am willing to
his call, My Dearest think
live is Christ, but to die is
... If you felt this ...
would not think I call
... thing, or wish anybody
into this world, And a...
... to night, I am goin[g]
... one that you ...
... in, I shall be
company ... have good examples
... but I hope I shall do
disgrace the flag under
... what is a year or two of

you, with the world's for
my pocket, with I see no
of obtaining at home, y[ou]
If we want happiness we m[ust]
it, and I don't care how ...
pay for it if I can bear a...
...'s of the bargain, and ...
with you, for My Dearest ...
shall never love another, ...
way to night and be hap[py]
knew you would be happ[y]
will always be a home f[or]
[w]henever you like to com[e]
is a great pleasure for me ...
But I shall not go before ...
like you, Dearest if you ...
see me happy ...
... be ...
... through the ...
Oh, how sweet will my evenings ...
While laying on the gentle heaven[s]
And watching the stars, as they twin[kle]
Thinking of home, an...

Scarlet fever delirium — Mary to James Richmond

Mary Richmond's husband, James, was often away from home in his role as a Member of the House of Representatives. In August 1865 he had just been made a cabinet minister and was in Wellington. Mary wrote to James on their wedding anniversary from their home in Nelson after nursing several of their children through scarlet fever. She was weak from the birth of her fifth child and writes as if feverish, with many crossings-out.

MANUSCRIPTS AND ARCHIVES COLLECTION, ALEXANDER TURNBULL LIBRARY
MS-PAPERS-4298-047

Aug 21 — 1865 Monday
Richmond Hill
Nelson

Your kind extravagant present has just come & pleases me very much — many many thanks for it dear James.

My own dearest James

Many thanks for your sweet kind letter. I cannot tell you how it has refreshed & comforted me — and I much needed comfort — for I have had a time of much anxiety with the dear children — I cannot tell you how I have longed for you, especially in the night when I have been alone nursing them & when I have felt sad & anxious about them — yet I am thankful you have been spared the anxiety & fatigue — Thank God they are mending now — so I can write happily to you on this our wedding day — Dearest James I am deeply thankful for your love — I feel quite unworthy of it — but still I am glad & thankful to accept it — I am sure it will help me to be better — I feel very peaceful today — rather weary & weak from want of sleep — & the fatigues of nursing — but full of great joy in possessing you & the dear five children ...

Following her letter James wrote to Mary on 14 September:

Dearest Poly,
I am grieved to let you be so long without such comfort as I can give in times of trouble. It must be in future a more cardinal point with us to remain together. It seems to me quite wrong to have parted whenever anxiety or danger has come upon us.

Mary died unexpectedly after a short illness on 29 October before James could return to Nelson.

Anne to John Wilson, 1837

Anne and John Wilson emigrated to New Zealand as missionaries. When the Te Waharoa's war broke out in the mid-1830s, John remained at their Tauranga station while Anne and their two sons went first to Thames and then to the Bay of Islands to be out of danger. In her diary, Anne wrote of the difficulty of parting with her husband: 'Called again to part with dear John. Felt the anguish of parting extremely painful; every danger he might be exposed to, magnified by a frightful fancy.'

In February 1838, Anne's fourth son was born. Towards the end of November that year she died of cancer, aged 36.

COLLECTION OF MAX ARMSTRONG

March 6th

My own loved John,

Mr Chapman has this morning come inland and has truly made me miserable by telling us the Southern news — how that Waharoa is going to Rotorua ...

My heart within me is desolate. I know my love will say — ah, my Anne why are you so unthankful? Have you not your children, are you not with kind friends? But what are friends compared to you my love? And who ought to share most in your troubles but me. I feel quite vexed with myself that I did not accompany you in spite of your wishes to the contrary. I have regretted ever since I lost sight of you and not till then did I feel the reality of your leaving me. Forgive me my love for dwelling on this. My hand will write what my heart dictates, though I fear my tears will render all unintelligible ...

Since I wrote this I discovered a small hard lump coming under my left arm and am decidedly worse. I think it my duty to tell you so.

... your desolate wife
Anne

> *An Arctic glass bear*
>
> *David Ludbrook and Alice Fraser lived together in New Plymouth from 1977. In 1980, Alice came to Wellington to work on a television series, and David sent her this card. They never had their 'summer' together: David was killed in a motor accident in 1984.*
>
> COLLECTION OF ALICE FRASER

A

Darling Hand, Dear Breath, Dearest Fire,
As I could not find a golden Tiger with a few black marks, I am sending you this Arctic glass bear. It is a vision of you riding to me in our dreams — Really and truly. But perhaps you will stay awake so you do not fall off <u>until</u> you come.

Fragile glass lady, this is not a sad or frozen person or picture. When I looked, it came to me as my own colour, aura of these blues.

This is not Winter is it? We will not be so old and cold; actually too old, post-mature, to feel absolutely for each other. These are our summers coming. Knowing neither of us should pretend to be Spring, I make designs and work so we will not always be apart. Liar am I that has only lived, breathed Spring with you. There is warm summer with blue blue sky soon.

D.

Hamley diary

Robin Hamley enlisted in 1916 and travelled to France with the 19th Reinforcements. He was wounded by gunfire at Messines, but recovered in time to serve with the 1st Battalion of the Auckland Regiment at the Battle of Broodseinde, Belgium, in the third Ypres campaign.

Robin was engaged to Dorothy, of whom he wrote many times in his journal. On 11 March 1917 Robin had written: 'I hope to get back from this war and that all our boys will do the same. Also that I am alive to marry Dorothy.' He did not return from Belgium. On 4 October 1917, he received gunshot wounds to the stomach and neck, and died two days later.

Hamley kept a private diary throughout the war, written in shorthand form until the final page. The final entry is addressed to his parents.

MANUSCRIPTS AND ARCHIVES COLLECTION, ALEXANDER TURNBULL LIBRARY MS-PAPERS-2499

121
endings

Dear D & G

Think I'm dying
Best love
don't fret
Tell Dorothy

Rob

122
endings

Hongi to William Yate

William Yate arrived at Paihia in the Bay of Islands in 1828 to join the Church Missionary Society mission. His tasks were to make a study of the Māori language, and to teach in the mission schools.

Yate was later dismissed from the Church Missionary Society because of his sexual relationship with several young Māori men and returned to England. In 1835, Yate published his book, An Account of New Zealand. Included in the book are a number of letters from Māori, including one from Yate's former lover, Hongi.

WILLIAM YATE. AN ACCOUNT OF NEW ZEALAND; AND OF THE FORMATION AND PROGRESS OF THE CHURCH MISSIONARY SOCIETY'S MISSION IN THE NORTHERN ISLAND. LONDON, R B SEELEY AND W BURNSIDE, 1835

NEW ZEALAND AND PACIFIC COLLECTION, ALEXANDER TURNBULL LIBRARY,

To the man whose name is Yate, and who comes to teach us here.

Here am I, sitting in the veranda of my house at Ohaiawai, thinking within me, that I shall not see your face again, nor hear the sound of your horse's feet. The soles of his feet, with you upon his back, will not leave a mark behind them on my ground again, til I am dead, and Patairo is become the head of Maungakauakaua. Perhaps I shall die; perhaps not.

You say you shall return; but I am thinking, no: you will not leave again your good country, for this bad country, and this very bad and unbelieving people. You will love your own friends more than the New Zealanders, and will not again leave them for this. These are our thoughts. We have love in our hearts for you.

We are not good to your going; we are not satisfied with the Buffalo for sailing from Wangaroa, when you are within.

Go in peace, Mr Yate, and see your friends in Europe; and say How-do-you-do to the whole of them, not passing over one. This is all, from him who was once your boy, but is now married to a wife at Maungakauakaua,

me
Hongi

123
endings

Shirley to Lester Lye

Shirley Lye writes: 'This letter was written by me to my husband shortly after Christmas 1991 ... and after writing and giving it to him I never saw or reread it until recently when I came across it amongst the papers of my husband, Lester, who died shortly after a stroke in September 1997. I had written it very hastily and with the greatest sincerity and on rereading it could not recall writing it but the painful circumstances were only too easily remembered.'

COLLECTION OF SHIRLEY LYE

Dear Lester

I'm writing this down because when we try to talk we always end in arguments or are interrupted in some way & to me its very, very important so I hope you'll take the time to read it all & hopefully think about what I'm trying to say ...

Last week after you had had your bad turn at the bowling club I felt we both realised it was a warning that our days, as we spend them now could be numbered, and I suddenly felt & thought you did also, just how much we have to lose in every way when they are over & also how much we still have to share & enjoy & I wanted desperately for us to be happy together ...

In the past Xmas has always been clouded with unhappiness,

unhappy memories, fights, arguments, separation etc, but this year even though I knew it wasn't what you would have chosen, or me either for that matter, we were so happy together, all that was behind us & I thought that finally we had found what was the only thing I have ever wanted, to be happy together in each other's company, accepting and loving each other without criticism — I felt ecstatically happy.

Then the blow fell and it was all over. The incident (the potatoes) that set it off was so trivial it couldn't possibly have caused you to walk away from everything leaving me so absolutely devastated — & I knew that what I thought we had finally found was just a glorious fantasy on my part & you didn't want any part of it and were looking for any excuse to get out of everything that that Christmas day stood for, for me.

With all the agony I've felt in the past over some of the things that have happened in the past, nothing has ever affected me in the same way — this time I feel there is no future to look forward to & I don't know what the answer is.

I can't and don't want to go back to our mere existence of the past with its ups & downs having had those few wonderful days and knowing life really can be what I've always dreamed it should be, it doesn't cost money, or need diversions, youth or company, just two people feeling right about each other.

I can't live with anything else, I'd rather be dead.
Shirley

Owen to Irene Jensen

In mid-1969 Irene Jensen was diagnosed with inoperable cancer, with a life expectancy of some two months. She was 63 years old. Her husband Owen Jensen, was distraught. As well as visiting her he wrote her a series of letters every few days during the weeks she was in hospital, writing the things that he had never been able to say to her. All his energies went into making sure she knew the depth of his feeling for her and that everything she wanted was granted.

After her death in November 1969, Owen gave his daughter Caryl the letters he had written to Irene, who had asked that Caryl have them. Irene was immensely proud of the fact that in spite of a marriage that was tumultuous and sometimes difficult, she felt loved and was loved deeply.

COLLECTION OF CARYL HAMER

Darling

I love you. Can I say it again — <u>I love you</u>. But love in the truest sense, love at its best, is built out of what seem to be inconsequential things, trivialities almost.

Do you remember the beginning of our marriage when we sometimes found ourselves out of sugar because neither of us was partial to sugar. Nor did either of us like milk in tea. We have always shared a liking for many small things; and dislikes too. More than this the sharp edge of differences quickens love, too ...

I know how much you love our daughter and our eight grandchildren but they will go on happily enough without us. They want us; but that is not enough. I would hope that you love me enough for us to go on together agreeing, disagreeing, and all the rest of it. But, much as my egotism might like to think so, this is not enough either.

These are things that should make you want to get better quickly, but there is something else much more important. In fighting things as you have you had to have enormous courage. You must have enough courage to take you further because so many — believe me, a great many — are moved themselves to courage, to a greater belief ... because of you.

Its not just those who have sent you flowers or sat by your bed for a little chit chat. I <u>know</u> by the many who have spoken to me, some whom you have never met, who have been enormously encouraged by your fortitude, who I suspect have similar problems of their own. What you are doing, what you will do, I think they believe they can do, too.

So you <u>MUST</u> succeed. And I promise you faithfully, that, as far as I am concerned, it will all be worthwhile ...

Happiness is a happening that takes us on to a newer world, to real adventures of the mind.

Let's be happy
Love
Owen

I was hardly a 'good catch' — Michael to Yvonne Edwards

Michael Edwards wrote this letter to his wife, Yvonne, when he discovered that he was terminally ill with cancer. He also wrote letters to his daughters, Anne-Marie and Felicity, and his grandchildren, all of which were to be opened after his death.

Michael died two months later on 26 June 1995, and on the following day his family sat together and opened his letters.

COLLECTION OF YVONNE EDWARDS

Dearest Yvonne

I just want to keep telling you how much I love you. The happiest moments of my life have been with you ever since we met that January in 1957 at Lincoln College. It was then that I knew that you were the only one for me. From then on my life has been wonderful!

We have shared a lot of pleasure and sorrow but the joy has far outweighed the grief. One of the sorrows has been your illness. In spite of it you have done wondrous things. It has been since S.L.E. hampered your life that you have done so much. The quality of our life together has been more than enhanced by you. All the major events of our life together have been initiated by you. No wonder that it would be impossible to find anyone like you again. It took me long enough in the first place to find anyone who would be able to cope with me.

The last years have been the happiest. Now that the children are off our hands we have been able to focus on each other and the experience has been great. I sound awfully constipated in this missive. I never was a good communicator and a lot of what I have wanted to say gets strangled at birth. However, this is all from the heart. You gave me two beautiful and talented children in whom I am inordinately fond. Their rearing was mostly yours and I basked in the glory. You were a wonderful mother who gave of her time and concern unstintingly and at some cost to yourself. In spite of that you developed yourself and, again, I was the beneficiary.

I look back at my life and would not change one little bit. I have enjoyed life with you so much that every day has been a joy. If I go before you you will find me waiting impatiently for you to share the next world with me. I have no regrets and although I expected little of this world I have been granted one of the happiest lives that one could ever have. You, my darling, have been responsible for that. I cannot even envisage a life without you. If I ever had even the tiniest of regrets it was that we did not meet earlier so that we could have had more of each other — though I feel I got the better part of the relationship. You had to put up with me!

Trying to put one's thoughts on paper I am finding difficult as I never was one to express my feelings easily. How does one translate a deep emotion on paper? I waffle on trying to express a conviction that there probably was no one else in this world but you who could have given me such joy in my life that I feel fulfilled and content. The inner self just wants to be with you and share the events both trivial and momentous, pleasurable and painful of the day. I wake up knowing you are with me and go to sleep content with your presence. Why you were able to cope with me is one of life's mysteries. I was hardly a 'good catch'. If ever my life could be granted again I would change not one jot or tittle as I had the best of all possible worlds.

My darling Yvonne you gave great joy to me and I was fulfilled through you. We shared so many things together that I find it hard to think of anything I did, or even wanted to do, without you. Words are so inadequate that I am feeling most frustrated but I hope you will get some idea of the ache in my heart when I think of you. I remember I had the ache during the time of our courtship when I was scared of losing you and again when I went to the conference in Israel and could not share the experience with you. It is with me now when I contemplate separation from you. I am indeed a hidden softy.

Normally when emotion is discussed I try to find humour so that I can cope with it better. I find it very difficult to do it now because I want you to know how much you influenced my life for the better and how much I owe to you. I have so much to say and find it impossible to adequately say it. I loved you from the first moment I met you and have loved you totally ever since. I have felt your love for me which sustained me over the years and gave purpose to my life. Every day is precious — and I have had over thirty-three years of them with you — and as many more as will be granted to me. God bless and keep you always.

Your loving husband
Michael

Go on in your ordinary life

This letter was written by Eliza Nicholson, dying of cancer, to her only child, a daughter living in India. The letter was intended to be given to her daughter when the news of her mother's illness was broken to her by her husband, Walter. Eliza died on 13 February 1913. Her daughter could not return to New Zealand as she was expecting her second child.

COLLECTION OF JENNY PERROTT

Waimea St, Nelson
Nov 11th 1912

My own Beloved Child, Dear of My Heart

Walter has just told you & you are up against the first big sorrow of your life & your universe is crashing about your ears. Presently you will begin to imagine all sorts of horrible things, but I want you to stop & let this picture sink deeply into your mind. It is a lovely spring day at home, there is a riot of roses outside, Leonie is pink & the red of Ards Rover are flinging their colour out on the sunshine, the big poplar opposite is heavy with leafage, out on the verandah the wisteria which has dropped its blossoms is putting on pale bronzy green leaves, the patch of grass in front is vivid & the white flowers of the rhododendron are showing.
Inside the drawing room — you know what a pretty green sunshiney room it is, your Morris chair stands just in the archway to catch all the light, the table is behind the door, the mantelpiece is a bower of blossoms, a big vase of dainty sweet peas Mrs Fowler has just brought in on her way to church, roses everywhere, the photos peep out between them. Just at the foot of the couch where it can be seen — on a chair is a big bowl of roses. Arum lilies stand by the chimney piece. Think of this sunny flower decked room & the lovely comfy chair.

Then into it comes your own dear mummie, she is a bit thin & she walks a bit feebly & perhaps there is a little more gray in her hair than you remember, but it is still bright & fluffy all round her face. She has on a pretty green gown which matches the room & she sinks comfortably into the big chair & puts her feet on another one, her legs are a bit thinner — but isn't that an improvement & she has on open work stockings & pretty shoes & altogether she doesn't look bad lying there. By & by Lizzie glides in, Lizzie is a dear, she is so nice to have about, quiet & thoughtful & dainty in her ways & caresses. She fixes up the flowers a bit & dusts the mantelpiece & tells of her baking trials & so on. Then Pearl Evans comes in bright & cheerful, strips off her waterproof — for there has been a shower, goes to the piano & plays for half an hour, Chopin Preludes & MacDowell things. Then she goes & the Man brings your Mum's dinner, do you want to know what it is, four little potatoes with butter, some stewed apricots & rice pudding & a tiny cup of coffee, then she goes & lies on the couch for a while & the Man smokes his pipe & they talk cheerily of you all & people & their dear funny ways — you know — presently Miss Lorimer comes in & stays for an hour & tells things interesting & amusing. When she is gone they read & talk & spend a very quiet peaceful afternoon till tea time, which means the thinnest of brown bread & strawberries & cream.

Then Ethel Webber comes in & tells of the three new rooms George is having put on her house, & her bargains in carpet & curtains & all sorts of common interesting things.

When she goes Mrs Ellis & Lizzie come & Mrs E is very vivacious & amusing & Lizzie puts in shafts of wit which are keener, &

then your Mum goes to bed, after a very placid peaceful day.

Now my darling that is a true description of last Sunday — there was no misery, no fierce resistings of fate, almost no pain. Of course I don't mean to pretend that every day has been or always will be like that, it would defeat my object if I did, but there have been & will be many such & as for pain — now I will give you Dr Gibbs message. He has been steadfastly from the first against my telling you, he is so sympathetic for you dearie, but the other day when we talked it over again, he said well perhaps you'd better, <u>but</u> when you do, tell her <u>everything</u>, tell her you are resigned, except for those you are leaving behind & tell her <u>I won't let you suffer much pain.</u> So don't you get imagining all sorts of fearful & unutterable things. Last week I had a good deal but I had opium pills to take & then he took measures which have relieved me very much, now I have had no pills for three days & only feel languid as long as I keep still, & as far as I can see there is not likely to be any difference much for weeks.

My poor darling, I am so sorry, my heart aches for you, but I <u>know</u> you will be brave for the sake of the little one you are carrying near your heart. That is why I was really glad when you told me she was coming, with the responsibility of that tiny life in your hands you won't fret & worry & give way to your grief. You are not to mope & shut yourself up. Go out as usual to every amusement and entertainment that comes. Of course it will be much harder for you not having the Boy, but that is part of the trial that has come to you & you must brace yourself to meet it. From the time we first knew of this over four months ago, the Man & I decided we would face it bravely, <u>and</u> cheerfully. We would not waste strength in resisting the inevitable, which in any case comes some day to every one of us, & above all that we would not treat it as something to be hidden up & ignored, no shadows of horror but the open sunlight of common sense and daily talk of what was to come. Believe me dear, it has answered. The Boy is not there for you to talk to, but tell some of your women friends & talk freely to them about your mother, it will be better for you. I hope we are doing right in telling you now, we have had consultations many & anxious over the question, but it is the last chance of the Boy being able to tell you & I can't much longer write long letters

to you keeping up the pretence that there is nothing wrong, especially now that I am not going out at all.

It seems to me Dear Heart that I have said only a fraction of all I want to say, & done that badly. But Oh! My beloved be brave for the sake of the wee one who is coming, it would break my heart if I thought my trouble would make the world less sunny for her, because her unconscious feet had been led by her mother's grief thro the valley of shadows.

Since I first knew & had to write letters pretending there was nothing, I have kept a diary for you, to let you see that our life these months has not been a horror, but same & ordinary & that we have got every bit of pleasure or amusement out of all that came our way & you must do the same.

Don't be sad for me, I have much to be thankful for, I have no obligations & duties & cares calling to me, but just have to keep still & be waited on & fussed over. I can't tell you how dear the Man has been & is, how he takes care of me & does everything for me & so cheerful & bright, & plans with me for the future — 'the ruling habit' you see — He is getting to be quite a good cook & can do all I need & keep himself & Colin going. Mrs Stone comes twice a week, washes, cleans, folds & irons the clothes & Lizzie has seen to the dusting & keeps flowers fresh in the drawing room. Mrs Lem is here nearly everyday, the Cook girls often, Mrs Evans comes at least once a week & brings me cakes or biscuits, Hilda makes cakes for us. Dora Judson comes & plays for me & so does Pearl Evans, so you see everyone is very kind & I am well looked after. I have plenty of visitors, more than I want sometimes, now the whole town is becoming aware of the situation, which latter is one of the reasons we can no longer avoid letting you know. Of course at first it was an overwhelming terrible blow to realise

I would never see you again, you know what you have been to me, the dearest most understanding daughter ever anyone had — & never to see Elisabeth!!!, but it had to be, & I set myself resolutely not to think of that part of it, & when it came over me to put it away & think or do something else. Making Elisabeth's garments has been a labour of love & a great help to me, but I can't do that any longer now. However, life drifts past me & there are many compensations, a great deal of the bitterness is past, I suppose it goes with one's strength.

How long this will last no one knows, we must just wait. I hope you will feel I have done right to tell you, it will be so much easier for me to write when you know & it will be sweet to hear from you, though both these are selfish reasons & I'd forego them for your benefit if I could.

Now my darling a heart full of love goes out to you, be brave & strong & cheerful, & go on in your ordinary life as usual, get every bit of pleasure you can out of it, that is the way you can best please me & reward me for any & everything I have ever done or borne for your sake, don't cultivate grief, throw it off & be happy. Oh! my darling be happy for your mummie's sake. It won't pleasure me to have you mourn for me, I'd rather you'd be happy. Goodbye my own Heart's Dearest. If I could, oh! if I could only spare you this sorrow, if you could only once have brought your babies for me to see & hold, it would not have been so bad for either of us, but dearie I am sure my love is big enough to wrap round you even when I am no longer in the world, feel it round you, think I am still there, somewhere, loving you. My darling my own baby. your mummie

EN

Peter Fraser to Harold Kemp

Janet Munroe married Frederick George Kemp in Scotland in 1903, and they had one son, Harold. In 1909 the family emigrated to New Zealand. Janet met Peter Fraser and moved to Wellington in 1918 to be near him. They married on 1 November 1919, less than a month after her divorce to Frederick Kemp was finalised. Fraser became Prime Minister of New Zealand in 1940.

After 12 years of tuberculosis, Janet died on 7 March 1945. On Janet's death, Peter Fraser wrote the following letter to his stepson, Harold Kemp, serving in the New Zealand Navy minesweeping the English Channel. It is less a traditional love letter than a moving tribute to the woman who had been so important to him. Fraser remained Prime Minister until the Labour Party was defeated in 1949, and he died a year later on 12 December 1950.

MANUSCRIPTS AND ARCHIVES COLLECTION, ALEXANDER TURNBULL LIBRARY MS-PAPERS-5614 (COPY ONLY; THE ORIGINAL IS IN THE COLLECTION OF ALICE FRASER, PETER FRASER'S STEP GRANDDAUGHTER).

Prime Minister's Office
Wellington
15 March 1945

Dear Harold

This note is a very sad one. In fact the saddest I have ever written. Words are not adequate to express my sorrow or to indicate what the departure of your mother means to me.

She passed away very peacefully in the presence of Rini, Mrs Armstrong, Miss Malempre, Sister Mary Margaret (who nursed her) another sister, the Rev. Mother, and myself. Her passing was just like the running down of a clock gently to the end. About an hour and a half before she died she said "Goodbye! Goodbye everybody" and her last words were to me, uttered when she was very weak "Darling, I am all right".

The expressions of sorrow and sympathy have been overwhelming. I am sending you a packet of newspaper cuttings. It is quite possible that I may be able to tell you personally all about your mother's death, the funeral, and the expressions of sorrow and appreciation of her life in a short time as I may be visiting London for the Conference preliminary to the San Francisco Conference ...

Alice endured a shock at Nana's death but she attended the funeral and I was glad she did. It will be an impressive memory for her future years. The funeral was most impressive — a marvellous tribute to your mother and her life's work. Up to the present some 2,600 messages of condolence have come to hand.

I must close to catch the High Commission bag. I may see you about April 5th. I will let you know through Jordan or Dick when it is decided.

I know how you must feel about your mother. She was the ablest and kindest woman I have ever met.

With love from all and hoping all is well with you.
Yours aff. P. Fraser

138
endings

Wild Flowers for Charles B

Ian Milner was born in New Zealand in 1911 and moved to Prague in 1951 to lecture in English at Charles University. He married a Czech woman and found it difficult to maintain his close ties with New Zealand writers during the 50s and 60s due to his working in the then communist Czechoslovakia.

Milner was a close friend of the poet and writer Charles Brasch, who visited him in Prague at least once. This poem was written by Milner on the occasion of Brasch's death in 1973.

MANUSCRIPTS AND ARCHIVES COLLECTION, ALEXANDER TURNBULL LIBRARY MS-PAPERS-4567-17

Wild Flowers: 1973

— for Charles B —

These wild flowers gathered where we walked
Last summer in the Bohemian hills
Bring unasked your voice your stride your look

I had not thought there could be pain
Like this bare memory
That you were here.

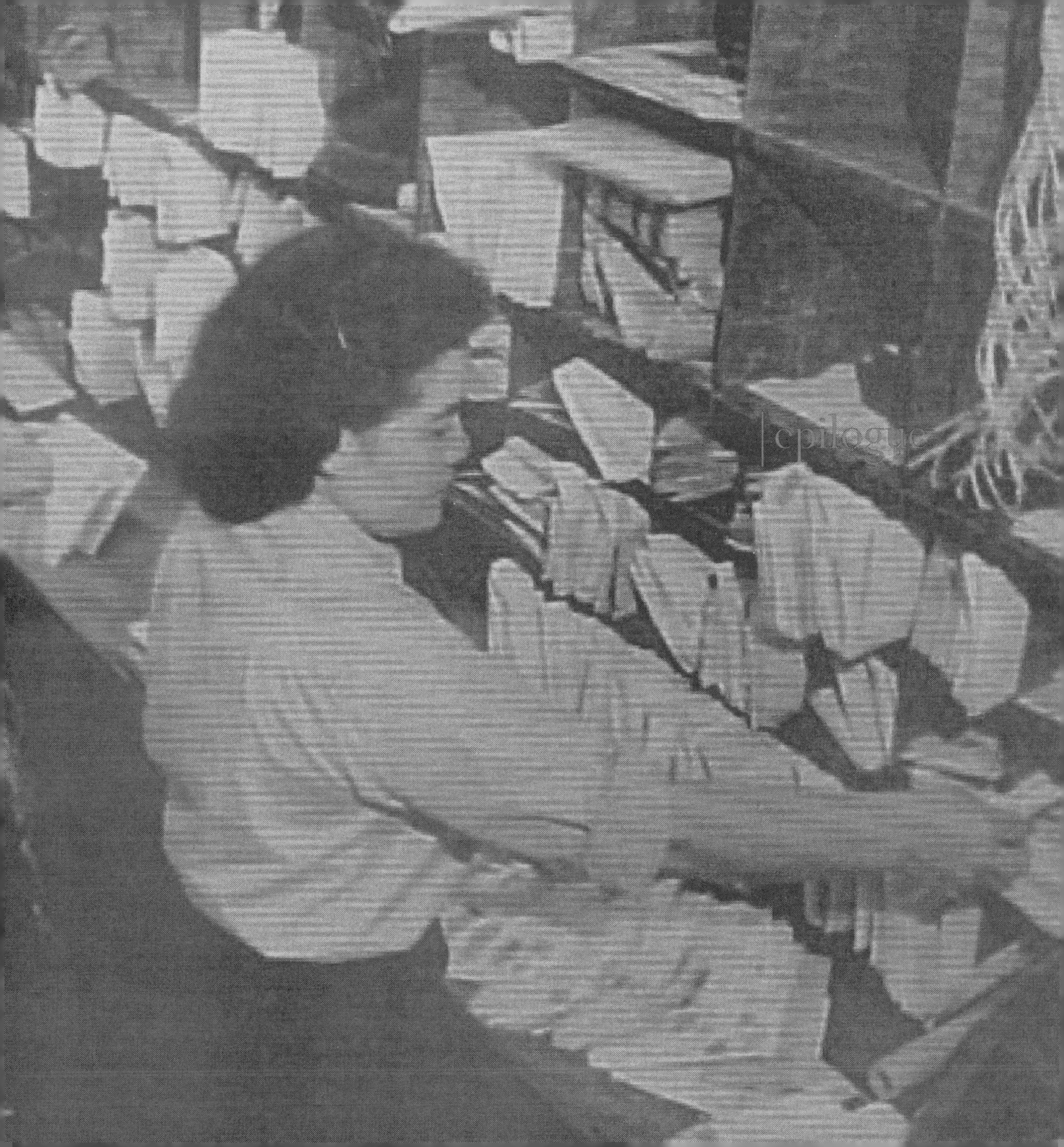
epilogue

On love letters — Mary Gallagher

Mary Gallagher was married to Timothy Gallagher and treasured his many letters. In this poem, written as a tribute to Timothy when he died on 24 August 1888, she notes the very personal nature of his love letters. Mary died on 11 October 1896.

COLLECTION OF JOAN CLANCY (NÉE GALLAGHER).

This is only a packet of letters
Tied with a piece of string
Only a trifle of memory
Fond recollections to bring

He who wrote them has gone to rest
God who gave him has called him again
Heaven knows and ordained for the best
He has passed from all sorrow and pain

To the ones they were penned, they were dear
Too precious and dear to destroy
There's a charm in each line, each letter and word
Which only this heart can enjoy ...

The words in this packet contained
Reflect what this writer has been
The purest, the fondest, most faithful of me
And honour thro' all may be seen

I have cherished these letters this life
Place them close to my heart when I die
They will smoulder to earth as I will
But beside me I wish them to lie

Mary Gallagher

Westport
Sept 30th 1889

[further reading]

Barthes, Roland, *A Lover's Discourse,* Penguin, 1990.
Clark, Margaret (ed), *Peter Fraser, Master Politician,* The Dunmore Press, 1998.
Fraser, Antonia, *Love Letters,* Penguin, 1977.
Lovric, Michelle, *Love Letters – An Anthology,* George Weidenfeld & Nicolson Ltd, 1994.
Meads, Rainer and Sanderson, 'Women's Words', Alexander Turnbull Library, 1988.
Orbell, Margaret, *Waiata: Maori Songs in History;* Auckland University Press, 1991.
Porter, Frances and MacDonald, Charlotte, *My Hand Will Write What My Heart Dictates,* Auckland University Press, 1996.
O'Sullivan, Vincent and Scott, Margaret, *Collected Letters of Katherine Mansfield, Volumes I-V,* Clarendon Press, Oxford, 1996
Scott, Jonathan, *Harry's Absence,* Victoria University Press, 1997.
Dictionary of New Zealand Biography Vols 3 and 4, Bridget Williams Books/Department of Internal Affairs, New Zealand, 1996 & 1998.

[endnotes]

1 (P. 11) For one of the first proponents of this idea, see Michael Goldhaber, originally published on the internet site, First Monday in 1997. Goldhaber also states that technology (such as that which goes into cyberspace) is shaped by the values of those who create it and it then helps promote those values, in the main, as it allows certain actions and not others. (*Reinventing Technology*, Routledge & Kegan Paul, New York, 1986.)

2 (P. 13) I have not included any of Mansfield's most famous letters to 'Bogey', John Middleton-Murry, which are all documented and recorded in the Collected Letters of Katherine Mansfield (Vincent O'Sullivan and Margaret Scott). Included in *Posted Love* is Mansfield's less-known letter to her brother Leslie in 1916 (see page 82).

3 (P. 14) Collection of the Alexander Turnbull Library, Derry Family letters, 1879–1937, MS-Papers-1043.

4 (P. 16) London, R. B. Seeley and W. Burnside, 1835. Alexander Turnbull Library, New Zealand and Pacific Collection.

5 (P. 17) Auckland Museum Library MS-93/130, Folder 6.

6 (P. 18) Manuscripts and Archives Collection, Alexander Turnbull Library MS-Papers-5586-02.

7 (P. 19) Ernest Hobbs to Lily Macdonald, Collection of Geoff Tilyard.

8 (P. 19) From a series of letters spanning 10 years from Thomas King to his wife, Mary. Manuscripts and Archives Collection, Alexander Turnbull Library MS-Papers-5641.

9 (P. 20) Antonia Fraser, *Love Letters: An Anthology,* Penguin, 1977.

10 (P. 21) From a private collection, Auckland.

11 (P. 28) Luit Bieringa, revised text of eulogy at Toss Woollaston's funeral, 3 Sept 1998. *Landfall New Series, Vol 6, No. 2, November 1998.* University of Otago Press, 1988.

12 (P. 28) Foreword to the book *Toss Woollaston: An Illustrated Biography,* 1990.

13 (P. 46) See Jonathan Scott, *Harry's Absence.* Victoria University Press, 1997.

14 (P. 104) Steve Gowan was flown to New Zealand by New Zealand Post, principal sponsors of the exhibition, 'Posted Love', that was on at the time of the discovery.

15 (P. 118) Between Ngati Haua, Waikato and Te Arawa tribes.